This storybook
belongs
to

_____

_____

_____

Stories written by Gail Cohen.

Figurines sculpted for the House of Fontanini
by Master Sculptor, Elio Simonetti.

Copyright © 1994 Roman, Inc.
All rights reserved.
No portion of this book may be reproduced
without the written permission of the publisher.

Published by Roman, Inc.
Roselle, Illinois

Printed and bound in U.S.A.
ISBN: 0-937739-22-7

# Nativity Stories

published by

**Roman, Inc.**

In Memoriam

## Nativity Stories

is dedicated
to the memory of
Ugo Fontanini

*"You enriched
the lives of millions
with your inspiration"*
1936-1993

# FOREWORD

Every Christmas, you, like millions of Christians throughout the world, celebrate the birth of Jesus — a simple narrative of just 20 verses in the Bible's New Testament...an event that has changed the course of civilization forevermore.

Your observances focus on the night Mary and Joseph arrived in Bethlehem after a 100-mile journey from Nazareth some 2,000 years ago. Their fruitless search for lodgings in a crowded inn is reenacted in pageants and immortalized in poetry and art. Their eventual shelter and the Child's birth in a manger, is recounted in great detail.

The Gospels eloquently relate the angel pointing shepherds to the humble setting of the Savior's birth; the three Wise Men guided by the Star of Bethlehem; and the Holy Family's return to Jerusalem.

These pages and the characters you'll meet bring you that beloved and familiar story in a truly unique and meaningful way — through the extraordinary subjects of the Fontanini® Heirloom Nativities. America's most popular nativity figures have been created in Italy since 1908 and are brought to you exclusively by Roman, Inc. In Bagni di Lucca in the heart of Tuscany, an area steeped in the rich artistic heritage of the Renaissance, these sculptures are crafted by artisans who have passed their skills from generation to generation in their families.

In 1908, when family patriarch Emanuele Fontanini sculpted his first nativity figure in his one-room studio, little did he know how his company would grow. At first, he worked with the finest painters and sculptors in Tuscany. With time, his sons joined him in crafting Christmas figures and decorations of heirloom quality.

Today, Fontanini Heirloom Nativities are acclaimed for their life-like sculpting, painstaking painting by hand and meticulous detailing. The cherished room has given way to a showroom and spacious crafting facilities to keep up with the demand throughout Europe and North America by collectors who choose only Fontanini when it comes to nativity figures. Now, a fourth generation of the Fontanini family carries on the legacy of devotion to tradition and excellence that is the hallmark of the House of Fontanini.

Many great artists have paid homage to Christendom's most celebrated happening with masterpieces in poetry, music and art. Foremost among them is the House of Fontanini master sculptor, Elio Simonetti. His 40-year association with the Fontanini family has been devoted to portraying the nativity story with figures prized around the world for their life-like sculpting and incomparable craftsmanship.

**The Bigger Fontanini Story**

Unlike others, Fontanini Heirloom Nativity figures tell a story reaching beyond that single famous event. The Fontanini family and Simonetti have pondered how this happening touched the lives of everyday citizens of Judea. Honest, hard-working folk then contended with many issues we face today: earning their daily bread...rearing children...surpassing disability... achieving recognition...overcoming pride...keeping faith strong.

When Mary and Joseph traveled six days to Bethlehem in response to a Roman decree to register for a tax in the town of their origin, they were not alone.

Their 100-mile odyssey brought them into contact with many fellow travelers jamming the roads to comply with the ruling Caesar's command.

The drama of their search for lodgings, the Child's birth and the magis' and shepherds' visits all unfolded amidst a bustling community of real people with jobs and families. Some of them were permanent residents; others had recently returned like Mary and Joseph.

How did they react to the news of the unusual events as it spread? Who else saw that fabled bright star? What did they think about the tales they heard from neighbors? Did they consider bringing special gifts to this newborn king?

To portray their stories, Simonetti's gifted hands shaped sculptures of musicians, shepherds and villagers — people from all walks of life during those biblical times. From his original wax sculptures, master molds were developed for the crafting of the nativity figures renowned for their breathtaking beauty and attention to detail.

The Fontanini nativity collection grew to encompass a colorful cast of over 60 distinct characters, each with everyday concerns and relationships touched by that first Christmas. And Roman, Inc. conceived the fascinating, exclusive Story Cards in which Gail Cohen relates each personality's fictional role based on intensive research of life 2,000 years ago. These exclusive Story Cards accompanying each 5-inch nativity figure breathe depth into the already life-like figures.

Now, these stories have been compiled in this volume in chronological order. They weave a wider-ranging, in-depth perspective of how people so long ago were touched by that famous first Christmas.

**Begin Your Fontanini Family Tradition**

You can choose from several sizes of Fontanini Heirloom Nativity figures to create the set destined to become your cherished family keepsake. Eight sizes ranging from the miniature 2-1/2-inch and the popular 5-inch to the magnificent 50-inch are available open stock, year-round to suit your lifestyle and home.

Creating the magnificent life-sized sculptures has been the crowning achievement of Simonetti's long and distinguished association with Fontanini. Countless people have admired these masterpieces when featured in the American box office hit movie, "Home Alone." Pope John Paul II enjoys them in his private Vatican quarters. Major European cathedrals in Brussels, Lucca, Ancona and Palermo display them to the joy of thousands of visitors.

With your Fontanini Heirloom Nativity nearby, gather 'round the family armchair. Cradle this book in your arms. Check to see that all the children — in your lap, beside you, looking over your shoulder and placing a nativity figure in the family set — can read along with you…and listen.

Now, take a trip back into biblical times and feel what it was really like to be living and working in Judea at the time of Christ's birth.

Once you have started your tradition, your family will always look on it as a special part of their Christmas celebration. We know you'll enjoy the world's greatest story as told by Fontanini.

**And when they had seen it, they made known abroad the saying which was told them concerning the Child. And all they that heard it wondered at those things which were told them by the shepherds.**
St. Luke 2:17-18

## *the story of*
# THE HOLY FAMILY

The night was slate blue with golden stars that hung from the sky as if suspended by little hooks. Cold air gusted as families across the Holy Land crawled beneath warm blankets.

Angels looking upon this barren region might have been surprised to find movement outside the city of David. Not Gabriel. God's archangel knew exactly who the sojourners were as they slowly traveled the expanse of the land leading to the gates of Bethlehem. The angel had been with the woman nine months before. He had delivered wondrous news with words of expectation.

Sitting at her home in wide-eyed innocence, the virgin Mary was told by Gabriel that she was to be the mother of the Son of God. The event was destined to change the world and the young woman was afraid, but Gabriel comforted her, and helped her through the coming months. He guided her soul as she prepared for the miracle.

Gabriel also spoke to Joseph, the carpenter, who was betrothed to Mary. Joseph needed to understand the mission his bride was to accomplish. And from the day of his enlightenment, Joseph joined Gabriel to guard Mary's health as she grew large with the Holy Child and wise in her newfound grace and maturity.

As the birth of Jesus approached, a census was ordered throughout the Holy Land by Roman Emperor Caesar Augustus. Law required that everyone travel to the city of their ancestors. Gabriel helped Joseph locate a donkey to ease Mary's travel burden and accompanied the two on their arduous journey.

Leading Mary over rugged terrain toward Bethlehem was a labor of love for Joseph. How tenderly he walked the donkey, glancing at Mary with each step. Her radiant smile assured Joseph that all was well, as a gatekeeper allowed the couple into Bethlehem, in the late night hours. He observed the woman's state of maternity, though Mary never uttered a sound, and pointed out the inn before returning to his solitary post.

Since only the stable behind the crowded inn could be found to shelter the two, there was no choice but to make the best of the situation. The couple moved into the straw-filled room. They would share the humble shelter with gentle animals, birds and the still sounds of the night. They would wait out the long hours of Mary's labor with courage and faith in God's will.

A hush fell over the stable as midnight passed. A gentle breath of wind extinguished the single candle. The animals stirred with expectation. Then the sky exploded with light and showers of music! Great chorals of angels could be heard. Each voice serenaded the tiny Child born on that night of nights.

## *the story of* BABY JESUS

From the time Mary first received news from the archangel Gabriel that she was to be the mother of the long awaited Messiah, she and her husband Joseph prepared for the miraculous day of His birth. Neither of the two expected the birth in so humble a setting as a stable in Bethlehem. But, Mary must have known that God's reasons were purposeful and important.

The Child was said to have been born during the night in the presence of the stable's inhabitants: oxen and donkeys and sheep and birds. The animals must have been surprised by the visitors, and watchful as the night's scenario unfolded.

As soon as the child was born, legend tells, Mary took on the grace and serenity of a mature woman. Leg-ends also tell us that her Son was a sweet and peaceful newborn, sleeping contentedly in a cradle fashioned of a feeding trough and filled with the warming straw that had also made a bed for His mother. She dressed Jesus in clothes sewn before His birth, which were lovingly carried to Bethlehem in anticipation of His arrival.

Jesus was said to recognize the first visitors drawing near to His crib: they were the animals who had given Him their home during the night. Stories passed on through time say that Jesus reached out and touched the ear of the donkey and the face of the oxen as if to thank each for staying near and helping keep Him warm.

In the days following Jesus' birth, shepherds followed a brilliant star to locate his birthplace. And wise men bearing gold and aromatics and jewels and cloth would come before His crib and bow to Him. The Child was said to have favored the poorest among them with a sweet smile.

The little family rested long enough for Mary to gather her strength. Then, the Bible says, the infant was wrapped in cloth and prepared for the trip to Egypt before arriving back in Nazareth. There, Jesus would grow into a strong, young man…all the while preparing himself for the journey that lay ahead.

## *the story of* MARY

Among the many members of the royal line of Israel... and indeed, a direct descendAnt of the great King David...was a simple and virtuous girl named Mary. Mary was raised within the close confines of her home, learning all of the tasks other young girls mastered as they prepared to become wives and mothers.

Mary had yet to turn 14 when she became engaged to Joseph the carpenter. Before the two were married, a miraculous occurrence took place that was to change the direction of their lives. The angel Gabriel appeared before Mary. The young woman was frightened, having never seen an angel.

Gabriel calmed her with a soothing voice and told her that she was to have a son. Gabriel's explanation was filled with joy as he told her that the Child would be the Son of God, and that He would be called Jesus.

When Mary told Joseph of the angel's coming, he thought, "How could this be?" But then God spoke to him, too. He became a tender and loving husband, comforting her throughout her pregnancy.

As Mary's term was ending, a decree was issued ordering all citizens to their ancestral homes. Mary and Joseph were forced to make a journey to Bethlehem on a frail little donkey...and by the time they reached the village, it was late and there were no rooms to rent in the crowded town.

Mary was tired and did not care that the only place available for the night was a simple stable. She did not complain, but rather rode the faithful donkey to the shelter and allowed Joseph to help her into the spacious, cold room. He was concerned about Mary giving birth in such an unseemly place. But Mary simply smiled and prepared herself for the miraculous birth.

As the night wore on, both Joseph and the animals kept watch over the mother-to-be. Suddenly, the stable's single lantern flickered and went out and in the night air arose a chorus of sweet music. Before Joseph could contemplate finding oil to rekindle the lamp, a wondrous star burst in the sky showering light on Mary. And in her arms, rested the sleeping baby.

## *the story of* JOSEPH

What sort of a man was Joseph, the man God chose to care for Mary throughout her pregnancy? He was virtuous and hard working…a carpenter educated at his father's knee. But he was also very kind. When an angel spoke to Joseph in a dream and told him of the son Mary was to have, he tenderly pledged to care for her and her child in the years ahead.

Joseph lovingly protected his wife throughout her pregnancy and watched in wonder as the child grew inside her. He became more distressed than Mary when word went out across the nation that all citizens were required to report to their ancestral homes for a census, but she comforted Joseph as he set about finding transportation.

It is said that when Joseph returned to his wife with the only animal he could afford, that he was ashamed and hid the little donkey behind his back. But Mary was not upset and indeed, she allowed Joseph to help her mount the beast and the husband led his wife to the city of David.

When the two arrived in Bethlehem, Mary's labor had already begun. Joseph was desperate in his effort to find shelter for his wife and had to settle for a stable behind an inn, for no rooms were left in the village. They repaired to the area with haste and from the moment Joseph opened the door, he felt discouraged.

"We cannot stay here," he said to Mary. "It is not a fitting place for the child to be born. I must find some other place for you tonight."

But his wife would hear no more of his plea and insisted that he help her to a soft place on the straw. Joseph stayed close to his wife. He placed clothes over her to keep the night chill away. And he unrolled the rug Mary had used to carry the child's newly sewn clothing.

As the night wore on, the single lantern giving light began to flicker and Joseph cried out that the oil was gone. But before he could consider going out into the night in search of more oil, a wondrous star appeared in the sky, lighting the entire stable and causing all of the animals to burst into a beautiful chorus of thanksgiving. And from the corner came the voice of Mary.

"Come see the child you have taken such loving care of, my husband," Joseph heard his wife say in a strong, clear voice.

## *the story of*
# THE GLORIA ANGEL

No figures in the Bible are as delightful as angels. They are wise in God's ways and gentle in their speech and actions. Angels burst upon events with a joy and understanding of man that brings us closer to God every day. Perhaps this happens because only angels are given special jobs by God that require them to associate with men and women on earth.

Angels bring a touch of the divine to all those hearing their messages and they're given responsibility for making all of the world's greatest announcements. This is the story of such an announcement.

Nearly two thousand years ago in the Holy Land, a decree was issued by the Emperor of Rome. All citizens were told to return to the home of their ancestors for a census. Among those returning to Bethlehem were a poor carpenter named Joseph and his pregnant wife Mary. The two traveled all the way to Bethlehem from a great distance with nothing more than a donkey to carry their belongings.

Although they did not know it at the time, God gave a small group of angels a special assignment to watch over this couple. These angels were pretty new, and still learning "angel ways". But they took their jobs very seriously.

Guiding the young couple over rugged terrain at the beginning of a cold winter, the angels did what they could to prepare the way. But even their best efforts were of no avail when it came to finding shelter for the two in the crowded town. They sang sweetly and used their collective efforts on behalf of Mary and Joseph but in the end, the couple was forced to occupy makeshift lodgings in the stable of a Bethlehem inn.

As the night's stillness settled over the land, an exciting moment came to pass inside the inn's stable. The angels assigned to care for Mary and Joseph flew closer to earth than ever before to observe the miracle. The fastest of the group swept over the little stable, catching sight of a newborn child through the stable's shabby, patched roof. And in an instant, the angels' mission became clear: The little band had been chosen by God to herald the news of the Messiah's birth!

With great excitement and joy, the lead angel of the little band broke into a glorious song that flowed out into the cobalt heavens and wrapped around the clouds. It was a song of thanksgiving for all mankind to share.

And their melody was heard to all the ends of the earth.

## *the story of*
# THE HERALDIC ANGELS

Every once in a while, a miracle takes place in Heaven: twin angels are born and the whole universe sings with thanksgiving. Two such angels came into the world on a winter day many years ago. They were beautiful golden-haired girls with different personalities. One, vivacious and high-spirited, loved to dart about the clouds bringing laughter to the other angels. The other, timid and radiant, preferred to sit thinking sweet thoughts as she strung garlands of stars into necklaces.

As was bound to happen, the high-spirited angel made one too many wrong turns as she sprinted from cloud to cloud. She lost her way and could not find her twin. Around the Milky Way she flew, searching for her sister. She asked all the angels if they had seen her, but none had.

Settling down on a well-populated cloud, the angel was never the same. Part of her heart had been taken away. Thinking she might feel less lonely, she tried stringing stars, but to no avail. Her strands lacked the patience and diligence strung into her twin's garland.

It came to pass that Heaven was preparing for a miraculous occasion: God sending a Savior to the world. Gabriel, a very wise Archangel, would deliver the news to the virgin whom God had selected to carry the Holy Child. His was a very important assignment and all of Heaven was on hand to wish him well as he left.

"Archangel Gabriel," the angel asked, "if you should happen to see my twin sister on your journey to earth, would you tell her I miss her and feel as though part of my heart is missing?"

Gabriel looked at her with great compassion. "Do not despair, young one. God tests all of us to ensure we learn patience and faith. Listen to your heart and you will find your twin."

The angel took Gabriel's advice. She helped other angels enjoy God's music by learning to play a golden trumpet. Her life became one of faith and direction.

As winter approached, all of heaven knew the time was near for the Savior's birth. Those who could sing practiced sacred songs. Those who could play music rehearsed with much fervor.

At last the night of the Savior's birth arrived. At the appointed hour, the earnest angel took her place and began to play the music composed for that night.

As the music progressed, a melodious sound came from the very center of the heavens. The angel recognized it as a trumpet like hers...yet the musician's style was sweeter and more deliberate. Had God rewarded her patience at last? Off the angel went in her quicksilver way of old...off toward the sound that was laced with stars and tied to her heartstrings.

## *the story of*
# THE STANDING ANGEL

Very few stories have been told about her, but an angel accompanied the Archangel Gabriel to his very first meeting with a young virgin named Mary thousands of years ago. Though she had no name, she had a very special job watching over Mary for all the days of her life.

At first, the angel watched over Mary's tranquil life thinking that Gabriel had chosen her for a job that had little import. But when Rome ordered all citizens to their birthplaces for a census, the little angel realized that her delicate mission would include overseeing a difficult journey to the City of David. She was determined to use all of her angel skills, reminding the young girl to rest before the journey and keeping an eye on Joseph as he sought a donkey for the long trip.

The journey began. Towns came and went as the couple pressed onward accompanied by the watchful angel. When Mary's wrap was pulled loose by a relentless wind, the angel came to her, tucking it around her body. There were two to keep warm, the angel reminded herself.

By the time the couple reached the gates of Bethlehem, Mary was exhausted. When the news came that no rooms were available at the village inn, the angel flew off to see what she could do. Her search was unsuccessful.

The angel returned to Mary and Joseph, finding them at last in a small stable behind the inn. Her heart was sad. How could the Savior be born in this place? But before she could begin to ponder this new dilemma, darkness came over the room. Not only would the child be born in this stable, but no shining light would welcome Him into the world, the angel thought.

She wondered whether Gabriel would think her a failure, but quickly dismissed the thought as a light shone brightly from the trough Mary and Joseph had chosen for the child's first cradle. Despite the circumstances of his birth, the Infant looked perfect.

She then looked at Mary and was filled with peace. For the angel knew that Jesus' birth in this little stable was determined by God since the beginning of time. And she knew that she had done her job well.

## *the story of* THE KNEELING ANGEL

Several thousand years ago, winter approached bringing a flurry of activity among the angelic chorus in heaven. Preparations for the winter concert were in progress, taking the efforts of thousands. Special robes sprinkled with stardust were fashioned of white. Wings were kept polished to glisten even in the dark, blue sky.

One young angel watched the excitement from afar with longing in her heart. She wanted to join the chorus, for her heart was filled with love for God and she knew that singing brought Him joy. But try as she might, the little angel couldn't carry a tune, no matter how hard she practiced. So she did what she could to help the other angels, tidying halos and smoothing out robes so they twinkled like a galaxy of stars.

When the pageant ended, the angels were weary from singing so loudly. They could barely fly and didn't know what to do when this important message was heralded by the archangels: Angel choristers were needed to go to earth at midnight, for a miraculous birth was about to take place in Bethlehem in the Holy Land.

What a quandary! Most of the angels were too weary to think about singing. Not so this little angel. She wanted so to add her voice to this special occasion. She prayed and prayed for an answer, and quickly realized that her gift of song to God was one that could not be held back.

Off she went to a private cloud, fluffing her robe and filling her head with every sweet thought she'd ever had. Then she opened her mouth and out came the most beautiful notes ever heard! Could they really be coming from her, she wondered? She sang again and realized that the songs came directly from her heart.

At midnight, God called out to the little angel. She went to the appointed cloud and instantly found herself dressed in a wonderful robe of shimmering blue. A blue sash was wrapped about her waist and a golden band tied her hair. Ready at last, the little angel flew with great speed toward earth, lighting beside a tiny stable. "Sing your song," a familiar voice told her, as a reassuring tap on her wings drove her forward. "You have been chosen from many to honor our new Lord."

## *the story of*
# THE THREE KINGS' JOURNEY

Independently, three men of wealth and nobility received a divine message to travel to a distant land to worship the Son of God thousands of years ago. Known as Wise Men because of their knowledge of the heavens and earth, these men were also rich in belief. Once they received signs of the Savior's imminent birth, each gathered a retinue of animals and prepared for the journey east.

The youngest king was called Gaspar. How his white beard flowed beneath an ornate turban! Layers of fine fabric fashioned his elegant robe, trimmed with embellishments of gold and gems. Gaspar came from India carrying a symbol of divinity: frankincense.

A Nubian prince named Balthazar journeyed from Africa to pray before the Child. Balthazar carried the most valuable treasure he could gather: myrrh. It symbolized the passion of Jesus and foretold His destiny. Dressed, some say, in desert robes and a cloth beneath his crown to protect him from the heat, Balthazar wore soft slippers so that he might not disturb the Child when he found Him.

Finally, the eldest Magi was Melchior. His hair was golden and long and his beard was beautifully trimmed as befits a royal presence. His red robes were spun of fine cloth and trimmed with white fur. Melchior bore a gift of gold for the newborn Christ Child…as gold as his hair in the afternoon sun.

Though each wise man left his home alone, a magnificent star brought the three together. It had shone brightly over their heads on the night of Christ's birth, adding to the urgency of the journey. Stopping briefly at King Herod's palace to pay their respects to the local ruler as was custom, the Magi completed the journey to the threshold of the Bethlehem inn.

Quietly, the kings entered the enclosure, joining worshipers and animals before the blessed Baby. Despite the miles each had traveled, they did not look at all tired. Kneeling to worship, adore and present the Child with the treasures they had brought, they stayed until the last shadows of the sun left the earth.

King Herod had requested a return call on their journey home, but a dream told them not to stop lest they endanger the Child. The three took a route far from the path of Herod's influence, traveling back to their homes in God's holy protection after their miraculous journey of faith.

## *the story of*
# BALTHAZAR

Of the three kings traveling to Bethlehem in pursuit of a wondrous star nearly two thousand years ago, the one who had come the furthest was said to be the Nubian King, Balthazar. This "Emperor of Black Men," who had journeyed north to meet his expected companions, is depicted in many nativities dressed in fine robes…but writers are uncertain as to whether his first meeting with Melchior and Gaspar found him dressed quite so elegantly!

It is said that Balthazar's journey had been so long and exhausting that his clothing was in tatters. And so we may conclude that he brought special clothing and changed before entering Bethlehem. Or perhaps his Magian brothers may have provided the attire.

Balthazar was indeed a prince of Africa and the King of Saba. Although usually pictured as mature, he does not have the wizened look of Melchior's face…nor the exotic facial features of Gaspar. Rather, Balthazar was the Ethiopian Magus whose gift of myrrh was brought a great distance with tender care.

Of all of the kings' gifts, Balthazar's myrrh was truly a gift of his homeland. Myrrh is an aromatic resin that comes from the bark of thorny, African trees. It was prized throughout the Holy Land 2,000 years ago, because it was said to deter vermin from invading the household when the plant was dried and pressed into incense. Symbolically, myrrh is said to represent suffering… and it was for that reason that Balthazar chose to bring to the scene of Christ's birth a gift of such meaning.

While Melchior, the elder statesman of the three Magi, was given the honor of being allowed to stand first before the crib of the newborn Jesus, it was Balthazar who was said to get the infant's first attention. Despite the gold and the sweet-smelling frankincense and the jewels and the cloth brought by the two wealthy kings, it has been written that the simple urn of myrrh carried by Balthazar awoke the baby Jesus. And he was said to smile sweetly upon the weary Nubian.

At the age of 112, on the day of the Feast of the Epiphany, Balthazar died after saying prayers at the temple. He followed Melchior in death by days and was buried next to the eldest king by their third companion, Gaspar. And at his burial, the youngest of the three Magi honored the Nubian by taking up some of the same resin as a sweet goodbye and showering the second wise man with the myrrh.

## *the story of*
# GASPAR

Gaspar (also known as Gaspard, Caspar and Jaspar) was said to be the youngest of the three kings following the brilliant star to Bethlehem. But youth is certainly a relative term when we think about the years of life granted by God as recorded in the Bible! According to most written chronicles, Gaspar was about 109 when he set out with his companions to greet the arrival of the Christ Child nearly 2,000 years ago.

Gaspar was a strong, proud king with the weighty titles of "Emperor of the World," "King of Tharsis" and a number of other, minor titles. Before leaving his homeland to make the Bethlehem pilgrimage, he was said to have lived in such splendor, that he sat only on pillows fashioned of gold-embellished tapestry cloth!

Although a man of many kingdoms, Gaspar was also said to be very sentimental. His favorite pastime was chanting the somber songs learned at the knee of his grandfather. Indeed, he sang the plaintive tunes to the other kings as the three made their journey to the Bethlehem stable.

This regal king is most often depicted wearing an elegant turban. Lyric poets have described Gaspar's headdress as wrapping around his head like a blossom of almond trees. We can imagine that it must have been fashioned of fine silk.

A beautiful vessel of frankincense was brought to the Christ Child by Gaspar. Writings conclude that this fragrant, African aromatic, known to symbolize prayer, was also laced with gold. Some chronicles include fanciful tales of Gaspar spilling a chest of diamonds before the Child.

Many details of the wonder-filled journey that culminated in the visitation to the Bethlehem stable are today lost in time. But scholars seem to agree that this "young" king (who has often been said to symbolize divinity) came to the scene respectful of the senior Magus, Melchior. In deference to the eldest king, Gaspar stood aside to allow the older man first place before the Child.

## *the story of* MELCHIOR

Legend tells us that Melchior, the king of Arabia and India at the time of Christ's birth, was a small, gentle, elderly man with venerable ways. King Melchior has the distinction of being the eldest of the three wise men visiting the Christ Child and his figure is always given the honor of being placed first before the others at the baby's crib.

Indeed, Melchior's appearance substantiated his position: his beard was long and white, in dramatic contrast to the crimson robes that were his signature color. But this wise man wasn't just a learned head-of-state with wealth and regal garments. He was also a patron of the arts with a soft spot in his heart for the harp. His greatest pleasure was said to have been listening to its beautiful notes hour after hour.

Like his esteemed traveling companions, Melchior was said to have waited a lifetime for a star to appear in the heavens. Once it did, there was no question but that he was destined to join the other two kings for a journey to Bethlehem where it was promised that the three would find, waiting in the holy city, the Messiah.

Each king brought a precious gift for the Child. Melchior carried a gold censer to the stable on the blessed day of Jesus' birth. Scholars wrote that he also carried silks and precious stones to Bethlehem, and in one tale it was written that Melchior literally rolled out these treasures before the crib of the infant.

This stately emperor was said to have lived to the age of 116 and to have had a wife and a child. His journey to the crib of the Christ Child completed a life-long dream that must have found him joyful beyond measure. For on the eighth day after visiting the birthplace of Jesus in the stable, Melchior was said to have gone to the temple to pray and then peacefully died, his mission fulfilled.

As they had been in life, so were three wise men together at the time of the first one's death. Legend tells us that Balthazar and Gaspar lovingly bore Melchior to his tomb on the day the eldest Magus died.

## *the story of*
# THE SHEPHERD CHOIR

In the Holy Land, as in many cultures, the birth of children was viewed as a miraculous gift from God. If the children were boys, a father was assured his lineage. Work and treasures would remain intact, a most pleasant thought. The house of Avron of Galilee was no exception. Avron and his wife Dinah had three beautiful boys in eight years, but Dinah's last child exhausted her strength and she died quietly after his birth.

In a state of confusion and grief, Avron buried his wife. He did not want to go on after her death and was too devastated to take the advice of his friends that he take a new wife to care for the children. The three boys were reminders of his loss and since he had no family to care for them, Avron made a decision rare in the Holy Land: he would find childless couples willing to make loving homes for the boys.

The eldest boy, Enoch, was taken to Beersheba. A second, called Eben, found a home in Jerusalem. The baby, named Elias by his new mother, stayed in Galilee, but Avron told the new parents that he had no wish to see him.

Years after Dinah's death and the disbursement of her sons, families across the land were ordered to return to their hometowns for a census. Enoch and Eben's parents undertook the journey to Galilee late in the year. An inn accommodated the two families, and it was not long before they met.

The two boys immediately became friends and shared stories about their lives as the sons of shepherds. As their parents stood in registry lines, the two were left behind to play games and sing songs. The innkeeper noticed that the boys' voices blended wonderfully together, and he asked their parents if the two could sing for customers dining at the inn. There was no objection, and on the following night, delighted patrons enjoyed their melodious voices.

The innkeeper pleaded for one more performance, and as fate would have it, Elias and his parents were present the following night. The third child begged his father to allow him to join the two, and soon stood beside the eldest. His voice was a perfect blend and the three sweet voices filled the night with joyous song.

The boys' parents were enchanted by the combined sounds of their sons' voices, and determined they would do what they could to stay in touch.

From that day forward, the boys were brought together often. As each of them celebrated important birthdays and other occasions, the others were always in attendance. Distance would be of no matter. And so began a lifelong brotherhood that transcended the bonds of blood and would never end.

## *the story of*
# AARON

**B**oys and girls of every time and culture love to pretend. In the Holy Land, children were no different. Outgrown clothing, while scarce, became wonderful costumes for make believe kings and queens. Small boys made swords from sticks, pretending to be adventurers and warriors. And little girls played mother, sitting for hours by the family hearth where they were often given real grain to grind in preparation for future roles.

Aaron's favorite fantasy came from an early experience. He had gone to Jerusalem's Fish Gate with his mother as a very tiny boy. The Gate was her final stop, as by the time they arrived there, she had animal skin bags filled with onions, leeks, garlic and beets from the marketplace. At the Fish Gate, Aaron took a few steps away from his mother as she bargained for the day's catch, to get a closer look at part of a huge caravan that had just pulled into town.

"What are those?" Aaron asked an old woman squatting on the ground next to the gate. She shielded her eyes from the sun and looked toward the huge beasts laden with decorated blankets and hung with saddle bags filled with provisions.

"Those are called camels, little one," the wrinkled woman finally said, having determined that the dromedaries were the object of the boy's question. "God's nomads take the camels out into the vast desert." She continued, "They can go for many, many days without water, and yet camels can give milk."

"Someday, I will have a big camel," Aaron said wisely, barely able to see the top of their saddles, for he was a tiny boy.

From that day forward Aaron's dream was to have a camel. He often went out to the sheep's pen, chose a small lamb, and pretended to ride into the desert on his sturdy mount, sitting atop a beautifully studded saddle. It was a dream that did not go away. For many years later, Aaron would grow to manhood and find employment with a caravan.

And although he traveled many routes and experienced all of the wonderful sights, sounds and smells of his journeys, Aaron's warmest moments belonged to the past. At night, with soft breezes pushing the flaps of his tent against the night, Aaron's first dream almost always began with colorful images of a small boy and his "wooly" camel.

## *the story of* ABIGAIL & PETER

Abigail's parents decided she would be sent to her grandfather's house in Bethlehem when she turned thirteen. The decision was difficult, but her bright mind needed more than their remote farm could offer. Further, Grandfather Peter's legs had gotten weak and he could no longer deliver the bread he baked to customers. Abigail's youth would be a blessing.

Forgetting her homesickness, she worked hard from the moment she arrived. Immersed in her delivery schedule, Abigail scurried from house to house, particularly on Sabbath eve. One busy day, she was almost knocked down by several boys racing from the Bethlehem inn.

"Do you have to run? I almost lost all of my bread!" she gasped.

"We wanted to see Him," one boy explained. "The Child. In the stable behind the inn. They say he is the long-awaited Messiah. Where have you been?"

The Messiah behind the inn. How could she not see for herself? Finding a window, she peeked in to see a man, a woman and a glowing light. The silence made Abigail catch her breath. She could hardly wait to tell Grandpa and was not prepared for his angered reaction. "I have no time, Abigail. Many say a Messiah has come…all manner of men claim the title. If you believe all of them you will spend your life making pilgrimages. Get back to work now."

But Abigail could not forget the glow. She returned to the window as she made deliveries, but did not mention the inn until one dark night when she awoke to hear her grandfather crying. How frail he looked. How alone. She walked silently to him and hugged him. He told Abigail he had been watching her sleep, sobbing that she reminded him so of his beloved wife. How he missed her, he cried.

"I am so grateful to have you here," he said. "When it was decided you would come to me I thought 'What do I need with a child around?' I am an old man and don't want to be disturbed. But now I realize that you are a gift to me in my old age. Forgive me for being so angry. My life has changed since you arrived. I am no longer alone and I am grateful to God."

Abigail, wise beyond her years, was grateful too. She would be Grandpa's helper always and knew the time had come to share with him the miracle that lived in her heart. "How can I thank the Lord for bringing us together, Abi?" he asked.

"I think I know," she replied, her eyes shining. Abigail filled her basket with fresh loaves and covered her head with a cloth. Handing Grandpa his walking stick, she said softly, "There are some miracles that cannot be denied. Come. Let us give thanks for each other."

## the story of
# ABRAHAM

Abraham was the quietest child of his entire clan. Despite the fact that he grew up amid so many sisters, brothers, cousins, aunts and uncles, Abraham never wished to change his shy ways. He would sit quietly alone with one of the family's geese or chickens, stroking the fine feathers of the animal until it fell asleep in his lap.

When Abraham grew to manhood, he took on all of the features of his distinguished-looking father: he was tall and slim, and his beard grew heavily on his chin. It seemed he had gone from looking like a sweet, young child to a mature man in a very short period of time.

But inside, Abraham never changed. It was painful to talk to strangers, so finding a profession was difficult at best. His father, brothers and cousins were all excellent tanners and butchers…many were Guild members and even officials of the Guild. But for Abraham, neither of these professions were possible because he felt a deep attachment to all living things and could not imagine taking up a career in which he would have to hurt God's beloved creatures.

On a particularly pleasant day early in the Winter Solstice, Abraham walked home from his new job as gatekeeper to Fish Gate, one of Jerusalem's busiest gates. It was here that fishermen brought their catches into the city's market and part of Abraham's job was to count the fish to ensure that proper taxes were paid by the vendor on his way to market. While the job was not very challenging, at least Abraham did not have to contend with slaughtering sheep.

And who could complain about a position that allowed him to be out in the sunshine each day? All of these thoughts crowded his mind on his walk home… until he realized that he wasn't walking alone.

Abraham turned to find a very thin dog. At first, the animal stopped and crouched, as if to say "please don't hurt me." But when Abraham bent down and then took from his leather shoulder pouch a bit of leftover kefir made from curdled milk, the dog's hunger propelled him toward the bearded man.

From that day forward, Abraham had a friend.

He called the dog Caleb, the Hebrew word for dog. Caleb followed Abraham to the gate each day and helped count the fish going to market. Best of all, the gentle, bearded man now had a companion with whom he could share his life. With Caleb's company, Abraham would never know loneliness again.

## the story of
# ARIEL

The water made splashing noises as urns reached into the village well to provide the precious elixir that kept alive the village's citizens. But the well was more than just a dispenser of life; it was the center of the community, too. Women came there to exchange news at its walls: an engagement broken; a parent's anguish; exotic tales of traveling merchants.

Among the women appearing each day was Ariel, the virtuous wife of Judah. Theirs was a joyous union, and the two wanted children from their first days together. With the seasons came fresh water to the wellspring, but despite their daily prayer no baby for Ariel. The sight of sweet infants lovingly held by mothers and grandmothers upset Ariel so much she began to draw water in the late hours of each day, long after a child might be brought to the well.

It was on such a late winter evening that she brought her urn to the silent square. Tying her jar to a sturdy length of rope, she lowered the vessel, listening for the sound of the water. So great was her concentration that Ariel was startled to find a gnarled, old woman when she looked up.

How frightening the woman looked! Black clothing. A face that barely peeked from the folds of her head cover. "Please, my child, will you give me water? I have come very far."

Sensing Ariel's fear, the stranger smiled sweetly, melting the young woman's heart. Ariel filled the jar quickly, removed her head scarf, and bathed the woman's face tenderly. She gave her water to drink from her hands.

"I will tell you something to reward your kindness," the wizened woman confided. "A child, unlike any other, will be born tonight in the City of David. You too will receive a gift you have long sought from God. I have come to be sure you are ready and ask only that you remember me, for I am your Tikvah." Tikvah, Ariel thought, closing her eyes. It was the word for hope. When her eyes opened a moment later, the old one was gone.

Ariel came to the well often over the next months. She came with the mothers and she greeted the grandmothers sweetly. But never again did she see the old woman whose late-winter prophecy was indeed a gift of God.

By summer's end, a child was born to Ariel and her beloved husband.

Throughout her days, Ariel knew that the spirit of the old woman dwelled at the well. Thus she brought her precious son Tikvah there each day so that they might stop a moment after their water was drawn to remember the old woman. The child born in the City of David. And God's wondrous miracle.

## the story of ASA

Asa used to beg his elder sisters to take him to the village well each time they needed water for cooking and cleaning. So despite the fact that water-carrying was "a woman's job," the sisters welcomed his cheerful presence and loved the fact that he could carry not just one water jar, as women usually did, but two, big buckets full!

Asa had a child's inventive mind. He borrowed his father's cattle yoke, attached wooden buckets, and delighted both the family and neighbors with his ingenuity. He could be seen splashing his way down the narrow, dirt streets of Bethlehem, dressed in his sheep-skin clothing, from early morning until late in the day.

One day, Asa went to the well to fill his buckets and found Susannah trying to fill two water jars instead of one. "You should have water buckets like mine," he suggested, helping the young woman hoist the well's bucket from its stony depths.

"Oh, Asa! I am glad you came. My neighbor's husband has died and she is old and very sad. She won't eat and is becoming sick with grief. When I went to see how she was feeling this morning, there wasn't a drop of water in the house. Who will take care of her now that she is alone?"

"Don't worry, Susannah," Asa said quickly. "We will make sure she's taken care of." He dipped the bucket into the well over and over, filling his buckets and her jars.

On the way to the old woman's house, Asa stopped to talk with his mother. She gave him some bread and some olive oil and a sweet made of chopped dates, honey and figs. They carried the food to the woman's little house.

It was dark inside the room…not a single light came from the hearth or any of the lamps. Asa could hear sounds of the woman's heavy breathing as she slept. He and Susannah lit the lamps quietly. They went about filling pots and jars with the water he had brought. They found terra cotta dishes and piled bread onto one and the sweet mixture onto the other.

Asa went out to gather materials for a fire, as the day was growing long and a slight chill was in the air. The old woman awoke to find a fire roaring in the hearth and what must have appeared to be a thousand twinkling lights from her oil lamps. Plates of food and a bowl of water had been placed beside the woman's bed.

She ate and drank, not knowing where the food and water had come from. But as though a presence were in the room, the woman felt at peace with the world, knowing that she would never be alone again.

## *the story of* CALEB

Even as a little boy, Caleb had to use a cane to walk. He was a sickly child who learned at an early age to maneuver about despite his disabilities. So, as his young body grew, new canes were fashioned to help him get around.

Caleb's family was very poor and clothing was patched and passed down to child after child. But Caleb never complained. He became his family's unofficial fruit harvester, and with each season, he took his hand-made basket and collected the pomegranates, mulberries, grapes and melons growing on the trees and bushes.

Caleb often helped his mother prepare foods because there were no girls in the family and his health required that he stay at home a great deal. As he grew older, he asked his mother if he could mix some of the fruits with honey and prepare dishes for the Sabbath. She found his request so compelling that she turned over the task of making fruit dishes to his care.

As holidays and seasons passed, Caleb's fruit dishes became favorites. Friends and neighbors often asked if he could prepare something special with their fruits on feast days. By the time Caleb had reached manhood, his skills were known throughout Bethlehem, and rarely were his health problems mentioned or even noticed.

Caleb's brothers sought careers as tanners and gatekeepers, but he preferred to stay close to home working on new dishes so that he could help his mother with chores as she grew older. One day, the owner of Bethlehem's largest inn came to Caleb and asked if he would like to work for him preparing food for the lodgers who did not bring their own on their journeys.

He was a bit reluctant. After all, he'd never much thought about working outside the family's compound, but his mother encouraged him.

"Caleb, you came into this world as such a sickly child. We never thought you would live. But your thoughtfulness and talent with all of the foods we have grown should be shared with others. You deserve success after working so hard."

And so Caleb became an accomplished cook. He took all of the sweet berries and nuts and figs and honey given to him by his boss, the innkeeper, and turned them into wonderful delights.

And his fame spread all the way to Galilee.

## *the story of*
# DANIEL

Daniel had to be forced to practice playing his pipe. He wanted to be working with his older brothers who imported wonderful things to the Holy Land. He listened to their tales over dinner, hearing all about new shipments of marble, spices, silks and ivories… each coming from some exotic place by boat and headed for the family stalls at several marketplaces throughout the community.

"Why must I practice, my father?" the boy asked almost daily, knowing he would hear the answer that had been told to him time and again since the first time of asking.

"Because your mother and I promised God that you would be one of His musicians, my son. Fever almost took you from us before your first birthday. As your mother sat up with you throughout the night, she heard the sound of a pipe playing on some rooftop. She told God that you would be a musical messenger for His word if he allowed you to live. By morning, your fever was gone."

Over and over the story had been told. But the boy wished that his mother had never heard the notes. Nevertheless, he did not dare disobey either parent, so Daniel continued to play each day.

The years of boyhood soon passed, and as part of the ceremony welcoming him into manhood, the rabbi had asked Daniel to play his pipe for the entire congregation. Again, he could not say no.

"We are so proud of the way you have prepared for the ceremony that will make you a man," his mother told him on the night before he was to be confirmed. "God must surely have wonderful things planned for your future." She kissed him goodnight as he went out into the courtyard of their one-room abode to practice for the morning. The moon glided across the sky effortlessly, as if to watch over Daniel in his last hours of childhood.

Early the next morning, as the family prepared to leave for the temple, Daniel's mother received an urgent visit from a neighbor. After an animated discussion between the two, she returned with tears in her eyes.

"Rebekah's little boy has lain ill for days and she was worried that God might take him," Daniel's mother explained, her eyes shining. "It seems that last night a wonderful song played on a pipe filled the night air and caused Rebekah's baby to lie very still for the first time in days. He actually slept. And before the sun came up, the baby's fever was gone."

## the story of
# DAVID

The night was cooler than usual, so David put on his cloak before igniting the lamp he used to check the animals in the stable behind the inn. A slight wind blew under the front door and sitting mats rustled a bit at the inn's entrance. What was there about the night that seemed a bit strange?

David's job had no real definition. He tended the animals and sometimes helped the cook. And often he welcomed guests when no one else was available. For a young man, he had been most eager to learn all about the running of the inn, owned by his favorite uncle.

On this particular night, the inn was filled to capacity with travelers, most venturing to Bethlehem to participate in the census taking. Men and women and children seemed to be everywhere, and the cook had even hired assistants to help get bread baked and soup cooked so guests wouldn't grumble.

David was very relieved to get out of the noise to the calm of the stable. He took his lantern and made his way through the straw slowly, watching the eerie shadows as they played around the huge room. In the dark, David could see the cows moving lazily against the straw and the donkeys settled into another corner. Even the sheep formed their own cozy circle.

For no reason that he could think of, David decided to clear the area at the center of the barn. He used his lantern to light hanging lamp wicks and then swept back the space with a sense of purpose that he could not identify.

The animals viewed him with no alarm, for they knew David well. He finished the task and then brought fresh water for them. Extinguishing the wicks, David left the barn carrying the single lantern.

A donkey, tied to the post at the front of the inn, indicated new guests. David entered to find a woman in blue wearing a white headcloth at the entrance. A bearded man talked with David's uncle in quiet tones, pointing at the woman who was obviously exhausted and carrying a child.

"David," his uncle called, "we have guests in need of shelter for the night. Although we have no rooms, I told them they might use the stable." The innkeeper looked apologetic, "I am sorry that I cannot do more for you. We are filled day and night these days…"

"We thank you for your hospitality in any case," the weary traveler said.

"Will you help them, David?"

"Gladly, my uncle," David answered, re-opening the door and then pointing the way with his lantern.

## *the story of* DEBORAH

Deborah sometimes thought that her entire life was being played out in the courtyard of her parent's home. Of course, courtyards were the center of home life during biblical days, but that thought didn't please Deborah much.

She longed to have the freedom given her five brothers and often incurred her father's wrath when she begged to be allowed to go to school…or even tend the sheep… outside the boundaries of her family's watchful eye.

Each day seemed ever to be the same. Deborah rose early since it was her job to collect eggs from her charges, the geese. Each one had a name, but she never told her family that lest they threaten to call a healer to give her awful-tasting herbal roots to cure her strange behavior.

She did love the geese. And she was glad to see them each day. Her basket was always filled with eggs after she collected them, and sometimes, Deborah chased the group around and around until feathers flew and her hair had come loose from the cloth she now wore to cover her head. It was part of her new wardrobe. She now had many scarves, gifts from her mother when she turned 13 just weeks earlier.

"You are now a woman, in the eyes of God," she remembered her mother saying as red, blue and yellow head cloths were presented to Deborah so that her head might always be covered.

It was late in the evening, but the child in the woman longed to say goodnight to the geese. Stealing outside, Deborah wrapped her head and grabbed her basket, as if to take care of a last minute task.

The full moon shone as Deborah tiptoed over to the coop to find her young charges asleep with bills tucked into the downy soft feathers of their backs.

One of the larger geese stretched up a long, white neck and opened an eye as if to be sure that there were no strangers threatening the group. He saw Deborah's scarf and was assured that everything was as it should be in the courtyard that night.

"If I had your wings, I would fly so far," she whispered, sitting beside the coop and taking off the scarf that reminded her that her childhood had slipped away.

And as if to say he understood her sadness, Deborah's friend arched his long neck and touched the tip of her hand before returning to sleep.

## *the story of* ELI

It was said that there were over 50,000 miles of roadway in the Holy Land by the time Jesus was born. And Eli sometimes felt sure he had traveled every one of them!

As a musician, Eli always felt important. He knew that music and song were important methods of communication and he particularly loved making up songs of thanksgiving and teaching them to the children.

Eli sometimes walked 20 miles in a given day. He had two pairs of long-laced sandals and a wonderful, hooded cloak, as the weather could change quickly from the desert's burning sun to the cool of the foothills. No matter the weather, he was always comfortable and ready to play his pipes.

The decision to become a musician wasn't difficult. Eli's father had been highly trained and was in much demand for feasts, weddings and holidays. And the son was no different. He had God's gift for making and writing music, and with his father's support, soon became a noted artisan.

Although Eli played many instruments pleasingly, his greatest talent resided in his ability to write songs. He composed so many as a child, his mother would often tell his father that their son would someday compete with King Solomon. And it was said that Solomon had written 1,005 songs in his lifetime!

Eli carved his own set of pipes of the finest wood. He used the many holes cut into each cylinder to control the pitch of his melodies and would often hold listeners spellbound as he entertained at weddings, his very favorite occasions.

"I am a most fortunate young man," he could often be heard saying, as he traveled the roads bringing melodies and words into the lives of the people in Bethlehem and beyond. "I have been given a wonderful talent that brings me pleasure… and also brings joy into the lives of others. My dream is to share this with my son. Some day. When I stop wandering the roads and settle down with my own family."

Then, off Eli would stride with his extra pair of sandals, his warm cloak and (if time had allowed a visit home) a big basket of bread from his mother. He tried to leave at sunrise, when the warmth of the rising sun set an easterly course. And if you were near the city walls, you could hear the sweet sounds of the pipe in the distance.

## the story of
# EPHRAIM

Ephraim stretched out on the grass, contemplating the sky. Though only 17, he was a self-proclaimed star expert, and spent much of his young life watching the heavens. Even as a tiny boy, he made up names and delightful stories about the clusters of stars he saw each night. Each was fanciful, evoking a beautiful picture in his mind of dancing images in a black night filled with a brilliant array of multi-colored lights and shapes.

Ephraim loved to share his sky tales with everyone. He told stories to the neighbors, but they were not interested. He tried his parents, but even they thought it very eccentric to name stars and compose stories about them. They regarded Ephraim as a sweet, unreliable dreamer and rarely asked him to do more than tend the flock closest to the family home.

On one cold winter evening, the boy slipped out of the house to enjoy "his" stars before going to sleep. Staring up at the lights scattered across the blue-black heaven, the glorious landscape captured his imagination. Soon, he fell asleep on the hard ground without even a cloak to cover his body.

Ephraim didn't know whether he'd been asleep hours or moments when he was awakened by a comforting warmth. Assuming it to be the morning sun, he stretched and opened his eyes only to be confronted by a magnificent star hanging right over his head! Beams of light lit up the land for miles around, and he jumped up in a state of fright.

His fear did not last long, for the star's golden glow soothed Ephraim's spirit. He quickly gave thanks for the phenomenon, just as he had given thanks for every other magical gift his eyes had witnessed. He lay down again to watch the star, lulled back to sleep by its pulsing light.

As dawn approached, Ephraim awoke to the real morning. Hearing sounds of activity in his house, he suddenly remembered the glory of the star and was eager to tell his family.

"I awoke last night to the most wondrous spectacle!" he shouted, startling his parents with his tone and manner. "A star, big as the sky, appeared before me…a true miracle."

"Ah, yes. A most wonderful star," his father nodded solemnly, shaking his head as he did each time the boy told a tale. "Let me guess. This one fell to earth and was made of solid gold. Ephraim, you must stop telling these stories or the neighbors will think all of us crazy."

Having heard this reply to his discoveries so many times in the past, the boy didn't argue. Instead, he smiled.

Then, he tucked his latest treasure into the deepest reaches of his heart and marveled, one more time, at having been chosen from among so many to witness a miracle.

## *the story of* EZRA

Even when Ezra was very young, he had a way with children. If a little boy or girl was sick… or maybe a little tired or hungry… parents knew they could call on Ezra. His quiet, sweet voice comforted the child and in just a moment, he or she was sitting peacefully, listening to a wonderful tale.

Ezra grew up and married. But he and his wife were never blessed with children. They had their own house and a big yard with all sorts of wonderful animals. Ezra loved to have the three neighboring children for a visit. He stopped his work and sat down (sometimes right in the middle of the compound) and began to spin a web of stories about the animals.

"Tell me about the chicken," they would shout. "And the geese and the goats. Write down all their names," they added gleefully, hoping to catch Ezra in a moment of forgetfulness. But Ezra would never forget the names of his animals and dutifully had one of the children fetch a stick so he could write their names on the dirt floor of his house.

One day, only two children from the neighborhood came to Ezra's mud house and both of them looked so forlorn.

"What is the matter?" he said to the elder girl. "Why have you come looking so sad? And where is your little brother?"

"He is sick and he cannot get out of bed. His head is hot and mama was up all night with him."

"I think he needs a visitor, don't you?" He put on his hat and off they went down the road.

The little boy was indeed sick when the three arrived. Ezra kneeled at the side of the boy's sleeping pallet and touched his head with his fingers. The movement woke the child and he looked at Ezra as if to say, "Why are you here?" But he was too sick to speak.

"The animals miss you," he said softly. "They asked me to bring you their love and to give you a wonderful gift. Can you see into my hat?" The boy looked into the empty hat and nodded his head at Ezra. "I want you to close your eyes and when you open them, you'll find a gift from your friends, the animals."

The little boy obeyed and when he felt Ezra's hand on his head once more, he opened his eyes. There, in the hat, were four perfect eggs. Gifts from the chicken, the duck, the goose and the quail.

"Get well, little one," the older man said. "You are missed."

## *the story of* GABRIEL

Gabriel, like many young boys, hadn't a great deal of patience for sheep tending. He loved more than anything else to daydream about traveling to distant shores, meeting all sorts of different people and eating foods he had never tasted.

Sometimes, when his mother had packed up his leather bag with raisins, bread, cheese, olives and a water pouch, Gabriel would take his lunch out and pretend the food was an exotic array of meats. After all, meat was very precious and usually only served at very special events such as celebrations and feast days.

And once Gabriel started to daydream, he was transported to a place faraway…and not even the sheep he was supposed to be watching were in his thoughts. He dreamed about all of the wonderful lands his uncles had described late at night when the candle light made shadows dance against the walls of Gabriel's parents' home. The boy was truly a dreamer.

On a particularly sunny day, out of the house he went and down to the nearby meadow. It was time to walk the flock to a different grassland to feed. Gabriel skipped over the rocks as the land sloped gently toward a familiar valley. He pretended to be a bird, leaping from rock to rock and lifting his arms to the sky.

Suddenly he heard a thud from behind and turned to find a small lamb wedged in between two of the rocks. Apparently the little creature had decided to follow Gabriel's footsteps over the rocks, rather than walking with the other sheep as they took the grassy route.

Gabriel shouldered the little animal. He grabbed his front and back hooves to make sure he couldn't jump down from his shoulders and injure himself further. Then he joined the flock for the rest of the journey into the valley.

Once a camp site was selected, Gabriel set about preparing the area for the night. Not once did he complain about the lamb's weight as he chose a spot at the top of a small slope to rest for the evening. He could watch over the small herd from this grassy incline. He set his charge down on the ground and checked his legs. The lamb seemed dazed but he didn't cry out in pain. He stood tentatively and then surely. And suddenly as he had fallen, off he went to join the flock with a turn of the head that taught Gabriel, even at so young an age, that we never know who might be following in our footsteps.

## *the story of* JARETH

Jareth loved playing his toy drum. He often imitated his father Abraham, the village's best drummer. Jareth pretended to play the family treasure: an ancient drum that had passed from generation to generation.

"Playing the drum is your gift," Jareth often heard his father say. "God gave you that talent, as he gave it to me," he added. Jareth nodded, but never truly understood what that meant.

Each evening, the drums came out after dinner. Then the boy was tucked into his bedroll beside the fire as his parents talked into the night. There was a comforting regularity to each night, until one particularly unforgettable event awoke all of the families in the town: A golden star appeared in the heavens accompanied by the soothing voices of angels across the sky.

Jareth was the first to awaken and he quickly roused his parents. All three wrapped themselves in cloaks and ran out into the winter night. Even Abraham, who knew much, could not tell his family where the star came from. Neither could he disguise the touch of fear that crept into his voice. The little family returned to bed, and despite the unusual occurrence, the boy's parents fell asleep.

But Jareth could not sleep. He wanted to know about the star. He wondered where it pointed and what he would find there. Assured of his parents' slumber, the child crept out of the house and made his way toward the very place the star touched the earth. To his surprise, Jareth found himself at an inn's stable. Standing on tiptoe, he looked into the window and was surprised to find a man, woman and child inside, as well as richly dressed men with gifts of gold. They placed them before the child and bowed before his little bed.

Jareth saw animals sitting quietly beside the baby and he marveled at the golden glow… just like that of the star… that radiated from the mother. Despite his young age, Jareth knew this was no ordinary child. He, too, must bring a gift.

Walking quietly toward his little house, Jareth's mind kept repeating over and over: "A gift, I must bring a gift." Suddenly he thought, "Your gift comes from your father."

In an instant, Jareth knew what he could give to the little child. His walk became a run, and his cold breath blew in billows as he approached his house. Working quietly so as not to wake his parents, Jareth changed into his very best clothing and quietly removed his little drum from the corner of the room.

Then, guided once more by the star and the voices, Jareth rushed back toward the stable bearing the most precious gift he had to give: the song of his fathers… a true gift from God.

## the story of
# JEREMIAH

Jeremiah was a righteous person. He believed every inspiring story written of God's promise to send a Savior to Earth. Each filled his heart with joy, and when rumors of a divine birth reached Jeremiah's village, he felt confident that the Messiah had come at last.

Unfortunately for Jeremiah, few villagers believed as strongly. Perhaps it was the hard life they lived. Or appearances, in the past, of other men pretending to be the Savior. Whatever the reasons, Jeremiah's neighbors lacked his faith. But that didn't stop Jeremiah.

"My brothers," he urged, "let us go to Bethlehem to see the Promised One. It is early spring. The roads will be easy to travel. Please. Come with me. This may be our only opportunity to be blessed!"

"You have drunk too much wine," they laughed. "If you keep making plans to visit every arriving Messiah you shall have no time for your flock!"

A discouraged Jeremiah returned to his wife. "Do you believe this is another hoax?" He was prepared for her nod, but Tirzah's sweet smile encouraged her husband to be true to his feelings.

"Do not listen to them," she counselled. "Listen to your heart." Her love removed all feelings of isolation and hopelessness. "I will see the Child for myself," he concluded, "no matter what the others say."

In the pre-dawn light, Jeremiah set out with food and bedroll after picking the gentlest lamb in his flock. Tirzah waved and watched them disappear over the hilltop.

Two suns rose and set before they reached Bethlehem. Tired and dirty, Jeremiah stopped at a well on the outskirts of town and was given a drink by two kind women.

"Can you tell me where the Child is?" he asked, half expecting the women to say "What child?" But God provided the answer. Both women smiled silently, nodding their heads. One pointed to a road, insisting Jeremiah drink again before finishing his pilgrimage.

His heart beat wildly. Jeremiah lifted the lamb into his arms, as though walking the little animal the final steps might be sacrilege. A sacred song came to him as the road narrowed. Jeremiah thought of the message he would surely bring home to his family and friends and smiled to the heavens.

There was no doubt. This was the highlight of a lifelong journey of faith.

## *the story of*
# JESHUA & ADIN

A son was born to Jeshua and his wife Sarai on a bright Spring morning in Bethlehem. Looking into his face, the two marveled at his trusting eyes and soft smile. Adin was the most serene baby either had ever seen.

"How content he is," Sarai's mother crooned, holding her grandson in her arms one evening. "When does he cry?"

"He does not cry, mother," Sarai answered, dipping dates and nuts into honey. "He is this quiet from morning to night." Sarai did not see her mother's brow crease as she left the house, walking purposefully to Jeshua as he tended the sheep.

"Does Adin cry much, my son-in-law?" she queried innocently.

"He is an angel," Jeshua replied, kissing Adin's head. "I tell Sarai we should have no more children. We have a perfect one." He turned his attention to a lamb bounding away from the flock, not wanting her to see that he, too, worried about the little one's silence.

The boy turned a year old the following Spring, yet nothing was said about Adin's silence.

A wondrous star appeared in the winter sky of Adin's second year of life. Angels spread joyous news that a child had been born in the inn's stable. Soon people from across the Holy Land traveled far distances to see the Child for themselves.

Sarai wanted to take her son to the inn. If the miracle was true, perhaps God would smile down upon her silent Adin. But she dared not go. To travel the short distance would mean talking to her husband about her worries.

Jeshua, too, heard of the miracle. But he could not broach the subject of taking Adin to the inn either. How would he explain his mission to Sarai? Fortunately, God spoke to Jeshua in a dream. The young father arose, gathering his son into his arms. They were halfway across the village before Adin awoke.

"Let's finish the walk our special way!" Jeshua whispered to Adin. He hoisted the little boy onto his shoulders just as the two approached the stable's opening. "We must be quiet," Jeshua said. In an instant, he realized what he had said. A shudder ran down the father's back. A single tear touched his cheek.

Adin hugged his father's neck with all of his might. He leaned forward putting his mouth against Jeshua's ear. At first Jeshua thought the wind had called him. Then he realized that Adin had said, "Don't cry, Papa."

## the story of
# JETHRO, TAMAR & SAUL

**B**ethlehem was chilly at Winter Solstice. Streets and alleyways were hard and rugged…but the children of the village welcomed opportunities to frolic without the swirling dust common to Holy Land summers.

A particularly adventurous trio were the children of Shedeur the tanner–Jethro, Tamar and Saul. Close in age, they were also close in spirit, playing together from morning to night. On this particular winter morning, the three lively siblings wiggled into scarves and head coverings as quickly as breakfast could be eaten.

Off they went to play Saul and Jethro's favorite game: caravan. Little Saul was always the camel driver, guiding his animals with a treasured stick he had found long ago. Jethro pretended to be a famous king. He filled a bag with rocks so the travelers would have gold and gems for trading along their exotic route. And Tamar was queen.

Sprinting through the alleys with rosy cheeks and giggles, the three raced around on their adventures. Coming to a low village wall, the children stopped short before an old woman they had never seen before.

She sat quite still and did not seem to see the children as they approached. Saul was so frightened, he hid behind Tamar's skirt. But the little girl was not afraid. She spoke sweetly to the woman, "Grandmother, do you need help?"

The little girl's words of concern reached the woman and she appeared to awaken. "No. I do not need help, but thank you, little one. I am simply overwhelmed by what I have just seen. He is here. The One the prophets have spoken of is here in Bethlehem. He is in the barn…at the inn." The woman's face grew soft as she told the children of her visit. "A gold star appeared in the sky…and too many angels to count. Go see Him," she urged. "Bring gifts, if you can."

The children backed away slowly, turning in the direction of the inn. Once out of sight, Jethro turned to his sister with a sigh, "We have no gifts."

"I have a song I can sing," Tamar answered. "It is a song about our people."

The thought inspired her big brother. "And I have a poem I can recite about my friends, the animals," Jethro added, excitement in his voice. The two looked at little Saul. What did he have to give, they wondered?

Both started to advise him, but before either said a word, Saul spoke up with great enthusiasm, "I will give my camel stick." He proudly held out his precious staff. It was his greatest treasure, yet one he would gladly give away.

Tamar squeezed her brothers' shoulders tenderly and kissed each of them on the head. "Let us go before it becomes too late. Our gifts will not wait."

## *the story of*
# JOEL

Joel was not yet 13 when his father died, and his mother worked hard to be sure her son had everything he needed. When there was not enough food for two, she gave the larger share of her meal to her growing son.

The legacy Joel's father had left was sparse. Clothing. A bit of money. Some land. And what might be described as the finest pair of sandals ever seen in the village. They had been given to Joel's father in return for an act of kindness and Joel was very proud of them. He longed for the day he could wear them and begged his mother to tell him the story of the sandals, over and over again.

Each week, Joel helped his mother by carrying her shopping basket to market. One spring day, the two arrived at the market and to their delight, they found a new stall that sold beautifully tanned leather items: belts, bags and other finely crafted treasures. Joel's mother was particularly taken with a soft leather pouch. She turned it over and over in her hands to admire the workmanship. Watching her face, Joel decided that the pouch would be his gift to his mother to show her how much he appreciated all of her sacrifices. But, how would he find the money to buy it?

The answer came quickly. A week later, Joel left his mother's side to bravely seek out the leather merchant.

"I have no money, but will trade you for something of great value," Joel said. "I will bring it next week." Joel had only one thing of equal value: his father's sandals.

He pondered about the dilemma as the week passed slowly and painfully. He hated the thought of giving up the valuable gift his father had left, but kept repeating to himself, "Is my mother not more precious than a pair of shoes?"

Finally, market day arrived, and Joel tucked the sandals inside his vest and set out at his mother's side. He waited for the right moment to slip away and approach the vendor, taking the sandals from his vest and handing them over. "Where did you get these?" the man asked.

"They were my father's. He left them for me when he died. I love them very much," Joel said, hanging his head because he was about to give them up. "My mother has cared for me even when she did without things for herself. I know that my father would understand."

"I gave these to your father," the merchant said with great compassion in his voice. "How fortunate you are to have a mother as good and loving as your father was. Young man, I cannot take your sandals. But I can give a second gift to a young man of such devotion and compassion." And with that, he hung the pouch over Joel's shoulder, handed back the sandals, and turned to a waiting customer.

## the story of
# JOSHUA

It is said that God creates in each of us a special talent that must be shared. For Joshua, that talent was music. The music that came from this boy was nothing short of miraculous. His parents hired great teachers and excused him from chores. Before long, he had become spoiled, intolerable and vain. While his music was sweet, his personality grew as sharp as rose thorns.

In late winter, nearly two thousand years ago, Joshua was to play at a wedding party. He practiced all day, donned his finest clothing and played his heart out at the wedding reception.

Once he had finished, off he went to the food table, heaping a plate with sweets and fruit. He barely noticed as two young men approached the table laughing between themselves.

"Yes, he is quite a musician. Too bad Joshua's not much of a brother. When Deborah and I marry, we don't plan to ask him to play at our wedding. I'm not even sure Joshua knows that his own sister is being married in the new year. He's concerned only with himself."

A chill went through Joshua's soul. He left the filled plate without eating a single fig, running out of the tent to the edge of the village. He wrapped himself up in his cloak of lamb's wool and self-pity, crying himself to sleep.

Awakening in the clear, crisp night air, Joshua looked into the sky and prayed to God that he might find a way to play his music so that his very own sister might want him at her wedding. Suddenly a golden star shone down on him. Joshua grabbed his pipes and shivered.

"Do not be afraid, Joshua," a voice called from the heavens. "I have come to bring great tidings of wonder on this night of nights. For unto us is born a Savior in Bethlehem. You shall travel to see him and play for Him as a sign of your repentance. And when you return, your brothers and sisters will see in you a great change. From this day forward, your music shall be your gift to the world and your heart shall rejoice."

On the very next morning, Joshua journeyed to Bethlehem where he found the Child. And from that day forward, his music was filled with love and sweetness…especially at Deborah's wedding.

## *the story of* JOSIAH

"Sometimes, I wish we had named you The Inventor," Josiah's mother often told her second son after he had fashioned some new object and brought it to her for approval. She loved this boy very much but was often afraid that his strange ideas would land him in trouble as he grew to manhood.

Josiah's creations were many! He figured out how to fashion the clay tablets young boys used for schooling in half the time they normally took by using less water and drying them on rooftops. He was the first in the village to apply the idea of large, underground grain storage jars to his family compound, and soon, Josiah had requests from many families in the village to place these jars into their yards. His popularity might have been happily enjoyed by both Josiah and his family were it not for the fact that all of these ideas were getting in the way of his upbringing!

Young Josiah was training to be a tax collector. It was the job his father held, and eldest boys were expected to follow along in their father's professions. And to add to this confusion, Josiah also loved music... sometimes more than anything else. So his spare time was spent perfecting "the ideal instrument". Needless to say, his days and nights were filled from sunup to sundown. And he enjoyed all of it.

One evening, with his father's tax rounds behind him and no requests for help with neighboring silo construction to hamper him, Josiah took out his favorite pipe and began to play. The bladder of a recently slaughtered sheep lay drying on the floor of the compound and it suddenly dawned on him that the skin was just what he needed to complete his project.

He knew he should check with his mother, but the evening was so mild and his desire to make this new instrument was so urgent, that he simply appropriated the bladder and with sinew and bone, he laced up the instrument and installed the two wood pipes.

The night shone brightly over the courtyard as Josiah completed the instrument. As he was about to try it for the very first time, a wonderful, bright star burst into the night sky from nowhere. The star seemed a brilliant miracle, appearing just as his quest to complete the perfect musical instrument was accomplished.

As if to salute the star, Josiah took a very deep breath and pushed life into the instrument. It sang loudly and sweetly into the air on that spectacular night.

## *the story of*
# JUDITH

Of all six daughters of Samuel, Judith was the youngest and the shyest. She clung to her mother's skirts as a little one, following her everywhere, as if afraid she would simply lose her one day.

"I don't understand why Judith is so different from her sisters," her mother would complain to her father. "The other five are so independent. I worry about our little one," she concluded sadly.

As Judith began to grow, she stopped clinging so tightly, but she still kept her eyes down respectfully all of the time and she still made a shadow of her mother wherever they went. She felt safe in their one-room home and was the best daughter of the family when it came to household tasks.

Judith could make lamps of olive oil with floating wicks to light the room. She became something of an authority on olive use, crushing the prolific fruit into cosmetics, soaps, and oils to be used in the Temple at worship. Her mother would watch Judith toiling over the press, humming contentedly as she went about her tasks.

One sunny afternoon, Judith was home alone making bread as her mother shopped for fish for the evening's meal. She reached up to the hearth ledge for the water jar and discovered it to be empty. Someone would have to draw water from the well and only Judith could do it.

Gathering up her hair onto the top of her head and putting on a cloth wrap, Judith hoisted the jug onto her shoulders and prepared to walk out to the communal well to draw water. At first her steps were hesitant, but then she realized that she felt all grown up and very proud to be able to surprise her mother with all of the baked bread.

She filled the jar excitedly and quickly returned home to the dough, once more humming as she kneaded the glutenous mixture.

As the sun began to set, Judith rose to greet her mother and help her with the fish.

"I am so tired, my Judith. It was hot and crowded at market." With that, Judith's mother went to lift the water jar for a cooling drink... and found it nearly full.

"I filled it up at the well while you were gone, momma," the young girl said shyly. "I wanted to be sure our bread was finished by your return. I knew you would be tired."

"You went to the well by yourself?" her mother asked.

"I am growing up, momma," she said, looking for all the world like a beautiful young woman.

*the story of*
# LEVI

Levi's life-long desire to have a son was destined to be an unfulfilled dream. He and his wife Hannah had five children: all girls. When Hannah died, Levi had no wish to seek a new wife and raised the five alone.

The job would have been impossible, he often confided, were it not for his sister Dorcus. She loved the girls as she did her own, though the five were not always easy to love! Abra, Leah, Shoshana, Ariel and Johanna each had their own, difficult personalities, and as the girls approached womanhood, Levi's problems grew. Their home seemed in a continual state of turmoil as the five bickered about everything. Levi took to staying in his fields late, gathering produce until he could no longer see the plants in the dark. He became so unhappy about the situation, he finally went to his sister for help after one particularly sleepless night.

"I cannot live with them any more! You must help me."

Dorcus assured him that she would find a solution. She told him to have the girls dress nicely on the following night and though he did not know why, Levi was comforted by his sister's soothing assurances.

When the next evening came, the young women had taken great pains with their clothing and hair and seemed to have stopped fighting for the occasion.

Soon Dorcus appeared, but she was not alone. A tiny, old woman wrapped in a voluminous outer cloak followed her into Levi's little house. The women were shown to mats as Abra prepared tea and the others sat quietly and respectfully.

"Very nice, very lovely," the old woman nodded, showing a toothless smile as she moved her gaze from left to right.

Pleasantries were exchanged, but no one dared ask who the old woman was, or why she was there. Then, almost as soon as the visit began, it ended. Ariel whispered to Shoshana that she thought this the strangest visit she'd ever witnessed.

About a week later, Levi looked up from his work in the fields to see Dorcus walking purposefully toward him. He lifted a nearly-filled basket of vegetables in one hand and his cane in the other, then hurried to meet her. When Dorcus whispered her message into Levi's ear he suddenly dropped all that he had in his arms and hugged his sister with shouts of thanksgiving to God.

As Dorcus had promised, peace came to pass. Over the course of the year, Levi went to the temple five times. Each time, he gave one daughter in marriage, until the last was gone. The matchmaker had accomplished her miraculous work. And the house of Levi was declared by the neighborhood to be the quietest in the village.

## *the story of* MALACHI

When Malachi was first taken as a slave in Northern Africa and sent to the Holy Land, he had another name…one given him by his homeland. But that was many years ago, and as the Nubian adjusted to living in Bethlehem, he became comfortable with "Malachi," the name chosen by his master. He knew his birth name began with an M, because his master selected the name Malachi when he noticed a simple, cloth bracelet around the boy's wrist with the letter etched and colored with wild berry dye. When his arms grew too big to fit the bracelet, he removed the band and placed it with his most treasured possessions.

Malachi was treated well, as were many of the slaves of his time. He worked in the mines and he became a talented and respected camel driver. Like many of the slaves brought to help build the Holy Land, Malachi found a certain dignity and glory at having earned his place in society. He proudly wore the earrings of a slave, a symbol of his station.

Malachi was fortunate to belong to a caring master. The man often asked if the Nubian missed his brother, since the two were brought to the Holy Land as young boys and were sold off to different families.

"I wish I knew my brother's whereabouts," Malachi would reply sadly when asked. "Family is very important and he was all I had."

One feast day, as families rested and visited among themselves, Malachi went to an inn that permitted slaves to congregate under a shady overhang of reeds. Several Nubians dressed in sailor's clothing were sitting on the porch talking of the sea. Malachi sat down and listened with half an ear until he overheard a seaman talking about how lonely it was to be in a strange land during a feast day.

"When I have time to sit and think, I often wonder what happened to my brother," he was saying, gazing off into the sky. "He and I were brought here when we were just boys. I don't even remember what his name was in our homeland, but one day I will find him."

"How do you expect to do that?" another replied, shaking his head in disbelief at the man's futile quest.

"My mother assured that when we left her as boys," the first sailor replied. "She made my little brother an arm band so I would never lose him. The band had a marking like no other: An M dyed of berries from my mother's garden."

## *the story of* MICAH

For Micah, keeping awake in the fields at night wasn't a problem. His mother sent him out each night with freshly pressed olive oil, just-baked bread, his favorite cucumbers and some sweet, dried figs. She filled a flask with water from a large urn that served the family, and packed everything in her youngest son's goatskin bag.

And each night she reminded Micah that he was very dear to her…as dear as the two hundred cakes of figs Abigail had given to David.

The nights were times for dreaming. As his family's flock rested in the cool air, Micah studied the stars and wondered about the life that lay ahead. His father was one of the enlightened. Micah could choose to go to school (not an option offered to his sisters) because his older brother would be expected to take charge of the family's sheep herd in years to come. It would all be very simple. He would learn a trade…perhaps as a baker. Then he could bring bread to his mother so she would not have to work so hard.

Micah heard a sound coming from the right of the herd and caught a glimpse of a young lamb, bolting from the group. The boy was a fast runner and had developed the habit of lacing his sandal strings all the way to his knees just in case that evening's duty included recapturing a wooly runaway.

How crisp the night air felt as Micah sprinted to the very edge of the meadow so as not to disturb the other lambs. Swiftly, he scooped up the soft-fleeced animal in his right hand while the creature struggled to get free.

"You mustn't do that again," Micah said gently to the animal. "You'll scare…"

Without warning a powerful light appeared in the cobalt sky. Shielding his eyes from the golden shafts, Micah tucked the lamb onto his hip. Even the animal quieted.

"What is that star?" he asked aloud. But there came no answer. The boy continued to hold the soft animal and to stare into the heavens, unable to move. Light poured from the celestial display, making the night even more beautiful than it had been just moments earlier.

And the star shone brightly throughout the night. Micah returned home the following morning, still spellbound by the miraculous sight. From his brothers, he learned that the heavenly display had signalled a great miracle that had taken place in the nearby town of Bethlehem: a baby boy had been born to travelers visiting an inn.

## the story of
# MICHAEL

Michael simply picked up his father's flute one day...at the age of five, his mother remembered...and by day's end, the small boy could produce some of the sweetest sounds anyone had ever heard. To encourage the child's musical interest, Michael received a 12 string lyre for his 10th birthday, and his entire family gifted him with a copper trumpet for the day he turned 13.

It wasn't hard to imagine Michael's joy upon receiving the trumpet... he loved music as much as he loved God for providing the sweet gift of talent. And he was too excited to sleep on the night of his 13th birthday, for as a man, Michael would now be allowed to play his trumpet during services at the temple.

Each Friday night, the men of his community would come together for Sabbath services. On high holy days, as many as 120 trumpets came together to sound the arrival of the Sabbath. To be part of that chorus was Michael's dream and he eagerly looked forward to playing his copper instrument.

Despite the fact that he played in such a grand setting, the boy favored the flute, his first instrument. Flutes were not allowed to be played in the synagogue, so Michael would walk out to the sheep late in the day and play new tunes on his wood and bone instrument. He might have imagined it, but it seemed almost as though the sheep recognized his songs and waited each day for him to come.

On one particularly bright night just after the Winter Solstice, the musician came out to the field with his flute. It seemed a particularly still night, though stars twinkled throughout the heavens and the air was crisp and cool.

"I must be the luckiest boy in Bethlehem," he said aloud, standing up on a smooth rock and taking up his flute. "This is a special song I have written to give thanks for all of the joy my family and music have given me," he announced.

The notes slid out of the instrument with a sweetness that surpassed anything the sheep had ever heard. Michael played on with a sureness that eight years had brought, eyes closed and lost in the music.

As time passed, Michael came to be known throughout the region. He regularly gave thanks to God for his talent as part of the temple's musical choir, and went on to greater fame as a member of the king's musical court.

"I thank you for giving me this opportunity to play for you," Michael told the king on the day he was selected. "You see my family has always believed in my talent and it is thanks to their love and encouragement that I am standing here before you today."

## *the story of*
# MIRIAM

The people of Miriam's clan...and indeed most of their neighbors... thought the young woman to be strange. Even her parents had long ago given up on any idea of marriage for her. Who would have her?

Miriam was a lovely young maiden, and she cared deeply for the animals belonging to her family ever since she'd been old enough to toddle out the family's front door. Playing amid the ducks, geese, chickens and roosters, Miriam hoped this happy time would last forever.

At about the time Miriam should have begun to learn to weave flax, bake bread and press olives, she announced to her family that she wished to become a shepherd. And since the family had no sons, there was no reason why she could not have that job.

"I don't know what I am to do about Miriam," her mother confided to everyone. Her father. Her aunts. The butcher. Even the rabbi. "Miriam won't learn to sew tunics or to grind millet for our breakfast. She's always running off to the field after her father and sometimes brings home sick animals. Once, she tried to hide a lamb behind the house. The geese went wild and my husband lectured the entire family into the night about Miriam's animals."

Miriam wanted to please her parents. She did everything her mother asked, learning to say the Sabbath prayers with her head covered and to embroider her sister's skirts. She even made the family's perfumes from gathered wildflowers and olive oil, cooking them perfectly and then cooling the scents down in small, clay vials. But her heart was with God's four-legged creatures and her family grew weary of looking for a change.

One day, as the winter solstice approached, Miriam wandered out with her father's herd in the late afternoon. She had just arrived, when she caught a glimpse of activity amid the herd. A small lamb had injured his leg and was limping pathetically as the herd pushed the tiny creature away from its midst.

"What happened to you? And where is your mother?" Miriam asked, lifting up the wriggling animal. She examined its leg, tying the extremity with the head cloth she carried in her apron. "I'm taking you home with me now, little one."

Loading the lamb into the big basket she'd brought along, Miriam grabbed a stick from the ground. Her father watched from a distance, shaking his head. She hoped he wouldn't be too mad.

Then, gathering up all of her spirit and courage, Miriam walked toward home with the basket against her back. And as if to say thank you, the lamb nuzzled her ear and slept.

## *the story of* MORDECAI

**M**ordecai had never been a happy child, and as he grew to adulthood, his personality grew more and more cantankerous. People suspected that his mother's early death upset him so severely that he decided never, ever to smile.

To avoid people, Mordecai found work at a Bethlehem village gate as night watchman. A lantern and a supply of oil were all the company he needed. He spent his nights yelling "Who's there?" from sundown to sunup.

All kinds of people came out of the night and Mordecai saw them all. The empty faces. The silent wanderers. Leaning on his crooked walking stick, he did his lonely job.

On a particularly chilly night just past the Winter Solstice, Mordecai's supper was interrupted by the sound of approaching travelers. He looked up to see a little donkey laboring up to the gate bearing a tired but beautiful young woman. Leading the beast was a decidedly older, bearded man, obviously weary from miles of walking.

Challenging their entry with his threatening stance, Mordecai leaned heavily on his rugged stick and lifted the lantern. Light spilled over the strangers.

"Shalom. We seek an inn, my friend," the traveler asked, letting go of the rope bridle. "We have traveled far and my wife needs rest…and soon!" he added urgently.

Mordecai moved closer to the young woman. Despite her loose garments, he could see that she was expecting a child very shortly.

The old man began to bark out his standard directions, but for reasons even he did not fathom, he stopped. Instead, his gaze remained fixed upon the woman. She seemed to glow with a shimmering aura of light, all her own.

"We are so grateful for your assistance," she said to Mordecai, smiling a smile that touched his heart. Her hand reached out from beneath the blue wrap she wore and rested lightly on his shoulder.

The gatekeeper was transfixed. He could not lower his lamp…nor could he speak for what seemed an eternity. Her smile continued to radiate until the little man felt his heart swell with warmth…as warm as the glowing lantern held aloft in his hand.

"Please, my lady, let me help you," Mordecai said, picking up the dropped tether from the ground. "I cannot stay away from here too long, but I will walk with you as far as the temple and point the way to the inn."

With that, Mordecai smiled a smile of the angels. He led the couple silently towards the inn. And when he returned to his gate, he was no longer the same man.

## *the story of* NATHAN

The villagers of Bethlehem all knew Nathan. There was not a child nor a wife who could not describe…in great detail…Nathan's comical orange hat and his wonderful, furry beard.

The children used to play guessing games about the man's age. But Nathan would simply smile his wonderful smile and refuse to divulge the truth. He would simply tip his head to the side (it was, of course the only part of his body not laden down with produce) and laugh.

"I'm many thousands of years old," he often said.

Nathan was truly a wonder. His wares were, quite simply, the best that could be found in the village. He sold lusty garlic bulbs, as big as roses of sharon, laced into flax-woven braid. And hand-woven bushel baskets of leeks that were said to be large enough to fight off the Romans!

Nathan's beets were fiery red. He often drew a crowd at the well or in front of a shop, boasting of the benefits of those beets. He promised miracles from the vegetables. And somehow, you believed Nathan's stories.

But the best thing about Nathan was his intuition. There were people in Bethlehem who really did believe that Nathan's knowledge of the village's citizens extended to the entire population. Perhaps the most often told story was this:

When the annual census was taken, a man named Matthew was required to bring his entire family… consisting of his wife and nine children… back to Bethlehem to be counted. There was just enough food to sustain the 11 for the journey from a distant province. They arrived with no family to take them in, and precious little to eat.

The family gathered together outside a courtyard the night of their arrival. They huddled together and waited for morning when they would try to find charity from kind souls at the marketplace.

But when the sun came up, the family was shocked to find, just a few feet from their cloaks, enough produce to sustain the family through the census period! There were cucumbers and grapes, melons and pomegranates. And next to the fruits, a heaping basket of leeks and the largest beets anyone had ever seen.

"It was the funny man, Papa," cried Matthew's youngest child when she saw the food. "The funny man with the orange hat and the beard. I saw him last night. Everyone was asleep except me. He carried baskets and he said his name was Nathan."

"Let us thank God for Nathan," said Matthew. And after prayer, the family ate their fill in the early morning sun.

## *the story of*
# RACHEL

**R**umors of a blessed birth were the talk of Bethlehem, but Rachel had no interest. The tales seemed far-fetched and shyness prevented her from investigating the whispers. "It's foolishness," she told neighbors when the subject arose. She went so far as to shop early to avoid the market prattle. This Friday Rachel had appeared at first light, her gathering basket awaiting the day's bounty.

Filling the basket, Rachel turned for home only to discover the road was blocked by an overturned pushcart. Chickens ran everywhere as the owner and other merchants chased the fowl. Arms waved. Birds screamed. Rachel sighed impatiently, turning to the alley that ran behind the Bethlehem inn. Midway through the passage, a sound stopped her.

"We have only today to gather food and belongings," a gentle male voice urged. "Once it grows dark, we must travel quickly. It will be a long, difficult night for both of you." Rachel leaned against the structure, waiting for his next words. But her basket bumped the wall, shattering the quiet. Like the chickens, fruit scattered everywhere.

Embarrassed, Rachel thought of running. But what of the food? She knelt, frantically restacking fruit until a man's sandaled foot appeared beside a pear. "Let me help you," he offered, kneeling beside her basket. Rachel steadied herself, blushing. She glanced quickly at his bearded face.

"You seem upset," he said tenderly, extending his hand. "Please. Come in."

Stepping into the stable, Rachel knew this was a holy place. Far inside the room, a woman in blue robes held a child. Soft light radiated from His head. Rachel instantly recalled the gossip that had begun last winter when angels and a golden star were said to have filled the sky. The women at the market… the awe in their voices when they spoke of this Child.

"Rest for a moment and drink some of our water," the man urged. "My name is Joseph. Please. Sit with my wife, Mary, and see the Child. We will not be here much longer." Carefully placing her basket on the floor, he took her arm and led her forward.

In that moment, Rachel knew that she would leave the best of her fruits as gifts in this man's hands… and she knew that she would help the family prepare for the journey they would begin that very night.

## *the story of* REUBEN

When people in the neighborhood saw Reuben, they rarely greeted him. Reuben didn't believe in foolish pleasantries, and lived a reclusive life. He believed that while people talked about brotherhood, few practiced it. Therefore, even Reuben's weekly journey to the Bethlehem market drew little notice. He simply appeared as usual, carrying his treasured knapsack tied around a hand-carved wooden stick.

Reuben had built a reputation for being picky at market. Seasoned merchants ignored his presence and didn't bother to tempt him with their wares, saving their speeches for those who would buy. But on this particular morning, a new vendor with baskets of sweet-smelling goods caught Reuben's attention by extending a rare invitation to sample his spices.

Reuben put his knapsack on the ground and dug into the reed containers, lifting samples to his nose. He loved the exotic spices, but in the end, would not allow himself to buy anything. Too extravagant, he decided, bidding the disappointed vendor a curt "Shalom" as he knelt down to retrieve his knapsack. But the bag had disappeared!

Reuben hunted through every stall and bag in the market, to no avail. Leaving without a single purchase, Reuben muttered that people would have stolen the clothing from his back, given the opportunity.

Arriving at his little house, Reuben threw himself down on the floor without unfastening his bedroll. He quickly fell asleep and dreamed of his knapsack. In it, the bag was filled with wondrous treasures and the dream made him warm and happy until he was suddenly awakened by the light of a brilliant star. It burst into his house and nearly blinded him.

Heart racing with fear, Reuben jumped up and ran to a corner looking for the protection of darkness. He found none. Then, just as suddenly as the light had appeared, it was blocked by the shadow of someone entering Reuben's house.

"I have something that is yours." A slightly familiar voice with an exotic edge came from the form. "I found it as I was closing my stall this evening. It took much time to find you, but I did not give up. I knew you would miss this."

Reuben cowered against a mud-covered wall as the figure of the man came to him and handed over the stick and knapsack. Then just as quickly, the shadow disappeared leaving only the bright light and the silence.

As Reuben bent down to unfasten the cloth, a rainbow of wonderful smells wafted from the knapsack. He sat down on the floor and by the light of the magnificent star, he opened the cloth. Out spilled grape leaf bundles tied with sinews. Each was a spice he had denied himself at market.

## *the story of* SAMUEL

If the citizens of the Holy Land were asked to name the most important members of society, they would probably select rabbis and farmers. One fed the soul and the other, the body. And while becoming a rabbi meant years of prayer and education, most farmers simply inherited the land from their fathers.

Samuel was such a man. His father taught him the many facets of farming. By the time he was 10, Samuel even knew the secrets of the olive trees.

"Olive trees are almost immortal once they mature," his father had told him one day. "They take 15 years to bear fruit, but they produce olives for hundreds of years!"

Each day, it seemed God's wonders would be revealed to Samuel in the fields and by the time he grew to manhood, he was ready for the responsibility of the farm. He married the daughter of another farmer and the two moved into his parents' home to begin their life together. As time passed, Samuel and his wife, Salome, had four sons and a daughter. He was a happy man.

But, although Samuel spent precious hours passing on the tales of the land to his sons, not one of the four seemed interested in the precious legacy of Samuel's forefathers. The boys grew and grew, and one-by-one, they chose the professions of carpenter, goldsmith, stonecutter and silversmith. Who would carry on the family farm, Samuel worried each evening when he returned from the fields. Who would tend the new olive trees and celebrate when each reached maturity and bore fruit? An aging Samuel would lean on the shepherd's staff carved by one son and ask God what he should do.

And, of course, the answer came. His beloved daughter Sarah came to him one evening as he returned from the fields covered with purple-red earth that had been freshly plowed to nurture barley and wheat seeds.

"My father, I know that you wanted my brothers to watch over your land and to grow food for the family when you are no longer here to do so. But each of them has chosen another path. Will you consider taking my intended husband as your son to care for this land when you are gone? I know he is not your real son, but our children will surely be yours and we promise they will learn respect for God's earth. Just as you taught me."

## *the story of* SETH

Like the majority of people residing in the Holy Land, Seth had a garden outside the city walls. He loved digging in the soil and planting his crops… and he particularly enjoyed harvesting fruit from the trees that had been in Seth's family for so many generations.

It seemed to him that the fruit represented the tradition of his family and that as long as the trees continued to bear fruits of the region, so would his family continue to live in health and prosperity in Jerusalem.

A special olive tree was planted for Seth on the day of his birth. It was a tradition among his clan that only an olive tree could be planted on the day of a son's birth. Olive trees had symbolic natures. It took 15 years for an olive tree to bear fruit, just as it took male children 13 years to reach manhood. By 15, many boyswere married.

When Seth went to gather fruit from the trees, vines and shrubbery of the family plot, he had developed a little ritual over the years. The last thing he did before shouldering his fruit-filled basket was to visit a moment with his olive tree. He gave it a small bit of water each time from his jug (olive trees require very little) and watched as the plant grew taller and taller.

One day, Seth didn't come to the garden by himself. He brought his friend Martha. This was the first time Seth had come with anyone other than one of his family, so the occasion must have been a special one.

Martha listened as Seth explained about how his father had planted his tree on the day of his birth… and now, both of them were tall and nearly grown.

Martha understood, for she was to become Seth's wife in the following spring. She loved the little tree and thought about what it would be like, as a member of Seth's clan, to plant a tree for her own son some day.

Seth picked up his basket, heavy with pears and pomegranates and figs, and started to walk toward the city gates.

"I will be coming with you in just a moment," said Martha, heading back toward the garden and the olive tree. She removed one of her headscarves from the pocket of her tunic and tied the cloth gently around the tree.

Then she ran after Seth.

## *the story of* ZACHARIAH

In the Holy Land, only royalty and shepherds were known to own dogs. Royals used them to help hunt animals, while shepherds valued them as watchdogs and sheep herders. It was said that the dog of a shepherd could be counted on to stay vigilant… even during long nights, when very young shepherds slumbered until morning.

Zachariah was such a shepherd. His dog was a gift from his father, and the two had formed a bond from the moment they met. The boy named his dog "Chai," for the word meant "life."

Zachariah and Chai spent their days with the family flock, working from sunrise to sundown. They helped to milk the sheep in the morning and often assisted the elders when they clipped the flock. Afterwards he, Chai and the herd would stroll happily to the meadow.

One day early in the Winter Solstice, Zachariah and Chai settled down to watch the herd graze under the late morning sun. A meal of "muries," a salty seafood dish, had been prepared by Zachariah's mother, along with honey cakes, mulberries and millet bread. The boy gave bits of his lunch to Chai and then Zachariah took a nap, knowing the dog would watch the flock.

Zachariah awoke to find the sun moving several hours toward the western sky. He called to Chai, but the big animal wasn't to be found. Walking into the herd, the shepherd studied the horizon…but no dog could be seen as far as the landscape stretched. This was truly a puzzle. The boy waited and waited, but the dog never came.

Zachariah returned home with a heavy heart. He could not imagine what had happened to Chai, but hoped the dog would appear the following day. When no trace could be found, the boy asked the people of the village if his dog had been seen. Many told him of a caravan passing through town, guessing that Chai had joined the wandering band.

Zachariah's days became long and lonely. He missed his friend and thought of him constantly as he took care of his chores each day.

One beautiful evening, Zachariah stared into the starfilled sky and wondered whether God had taken Chai to heaven. Suddenly, a huge, wonderful star… unlike any ever seen in the sky… appeared. It shone down over the pasture and made the sheep glow in the darkness. Zachariah stood and stared at the sight, noticing a small, moving creature directly in the path of the star's light. It moved slowly in his direction… and then faster. And the light bathed the two friends as they bridged the distance in the meadow.

## *the story of*
# THE SHEEP

The raising of sheep was a critical part of the Holy Land's social and agricultural system centuries ago. Sheep provided clothing, food, even milk… and were part of the intricate sacrificial system that governed religious life at the time of Christ's birth. Scholars have found over 500 references to sheep in the New Testament!

Spring was lambing season. About a month after lambing, adult sheep were shorn in the midst of celebratory feasting and dancing. By autumn, the pastures were stripped bare. Careful to avoid grain fields where crops were nearing harvest, shepherds led their ewes, rams and lambs about the countryside.

Although sheep have been depicted through the ages as being meek or bashful, a more apt description might be gentle and loving… vulnerable and dependent upon their shepherd masters. Shepherds' tales, passed down through time, describe the tender and affectionate nature of these loving animals.

Maybe it was because shepherds spent many solitary hours in the fields with their flocks that these particular animals bonded so closely to man… or perhaps God simply gave sheep a special gift of understanding that still exists between the two today.

## *the story of*
# THE SEATED CAMEL

The little caravan traveled to a distant oasis led by a proud camel. He knew the route and was accompanied by his eldest offspring, who was on his very first caravan.

Entering the grove, the driver removed empty drinking vessels and ran to the well. "We must move on," he shouted.

"But what if the nearest well has no water either?" asked another man. A loud argument was settled in favor of leaving.

Surely a long night's trip without water was unwise, thought the little camel. The elder animal must have agreed, for he sat down in the sand followed by the others and refused to budge.

Midnight arrived and the lead camel saw a golden burst of celebration filling the sky. An angel hovered above and told of a Savior born in Bethlehem. The young camel looked upon his father's face. Had his father known all along that a miracle would take place during the night?

Morning came. The men awoke and instantly remembered their dilemma. Frantically they tried to get the camels up… until they heard the sound. Water. The well was filled nearly to the brim. And the camels watched as the men rejoiced.

## *the story of* THE OX

He was the smallest of his herd… a tiny, almost lifeless baby animal, born in the spring of a particularly hard year. When his mother's owner inspected this newborn and discovered that he was a male, great care was given to assure his survival. You see, oxen were valuable beasts nearly two thousand years ago. And this fragile baby would be treasured by his owner, an innkeeper in the city of Bethlehem.

Because of the tender care given the ox, he survived the spring. His owners looked forward to the day he would take on the most important jobs: pulling a plow through the wheat…making sure threshing sheds were moved from place to place…and (if he was a very strong animal) perhaps operating a water wheel. His future was very bright.

But as the fall moved the Holy Land from a sun-drenched desert to a wind-swept terrain in anticipation of winter, the little ox began to show signs that his difficult birth had taken a toll on his health. He wasn't growing quite as rapidly as the other oxen born at about the same time. And his owner thought and thought about whether to sacrifice the animal before more precious grain and water were used up by an ox that might never work for the family.

Fortunately for the ox, the innkeeper's son cried and pleaded for his life… and his father listened. "We will wait out the winter and see if the beast rallies," he told the boy, tethering the ox to the inside of the stable. Sadly, the ox understood that his time might be limited. On a late, winter night, the darkness of the stable was interrupted by two travelers. From the ox's vantage point at the edge of the stable, it appeared that the man and the woman were about to take up residence. He watched intently as the man worked diligently to make a place on the straw for the woman and tried to understand their whispers and haste.

A short while later, the stable's only lantern went out. When the glow returned, the ox thought he saw movement from what had been the trough he and his fellow animals fed from each day. Up on his legs rose the ox, walking with great caution toward the two (almost expecting to be driven back by the couple's words).

But they allowed him to come, and over the edge of the makeshift cradle, the ox saw a sleeping baby wrapped in light cloths in that cold stable.

"This baby must be kept warm," thought the ox, as he gathered all of his courage and inched toward the crib. Closer and closer to the child he moved, his warmth radiating toward the little one. And as if to reward so great an effort, the baby opened his eyes and gently touched the ox's face.

## *the story of*
# THE DONKEY

Two thousand years ago in the city of Bethlehem, a little donkey was born. He looked just like other donkeys. Long, brown ears, sincere, chocolate eyes and a sway back. But, that's where resemblances ended. You see, this donkey was born with a vision of the future that included a brotherhood of man and animals.

Because philosophy was an activity that was supposed to be reserved for man, this donkey had a difficult time of it. To his masters, it appeared that the donkey didn't want to work. But in reality, he would simply stop to ponder an unkind word or deed and to wonder why people and animals didn't treat each other with love and respect.

Most donkeys don't concern themselves with such matters, so it wasn't long before other animals were anxious to avoid him (as were a series of owners). He was puzzled. Couldn't everyone sense that his thoughts were of lofty images and new philosophies… theories of how man and animal could work together for a better world? He brayed in his very best voice, but the other animals just laughed.

By winter, the donkey came to live with the keeper of an inn located at the very heart of Bethlehem. When the other animals housed in the innkeeper's stable wouldn't socialize with him (they all thought him peculiar and let him sit by himself day after day), he spent his time in solitude. Then, late one night, he was awakened by strangers moving into the stable. All of the animals began to buzz with excitement, but curiosity turned to alarm when the only light in the stable disappeared.

When the lantern was re-lit, strange sounds came from the corner. All of the donkey's stable mates moved toward the corner where a great light radiated from its center. The donkey very much wanted to see what had caused the excitement…but his heart was filled with sadness. It seemed that once again, no one wanted to share the moment with him.

Just as he started to put his head down onto the straw, the donkey heard a sound coming from the corner. The sound was music. And there were beautiful words about how all of God's creatures must love and honor one another. Perhaps he was mistaken, but it seemed that the words came from the stable's trough, now the resting place of a little baby!

All of the animals: the ox, the sheep… even the birds, came to the donkey and invited him over to the crib, where voices of angels continued to sing of peace and love among all of God's creatures. And as if he were the guest of honor at a splendid banquet, so the little donkey was escorted across the stable by his newfound friends… all of whom had finally come to understand their brother's vision.

## *the story of*
# THE HORSE

The caravan approached King Herod's residence on a dark night several thousand years ago so that its leader might beg for a resting place outside the royal compound. Since it was very late, the guard knew little harm could come of the gesture. He warned the entourage to move on before first light, then turned his back on them in the darkness.

When the sun came up, the gatekeeper looked outside the wall to be sure the caravan had moved on. Imagine his surprise when he found that all the animals and men had vanished, but a single, grey horse remained behind. The beast stood untethered and weary, as though ridden too many miles without a rest.

Horses were as valuable as gold during that era and the guard thought himself a most fortunate man… until he attempted to walk the horse. The poor creature limped so horridly, the man dropped its reins and walked away shaking his head.

The Three Wise Men approached Herod's residence that same day. They had come to pay respects on their way to a miraculous birth in the City of David. Tethering their beasts inside the compound, they stayed a short time to accept Herod's hospitality before taking leave. They were about to head east when Melchior, the eldest, noticed the grey horse standing alone. Dismounting, he walked toward it.

"He is not fit to ride, master," the gatekeeper told him. The warning went unheeded as Melchior approached the animal. He stroked the animal's side and discovered the dirt on the horse's coat.

"Please bring water and wash this animal," Melchior asked quietly. Too afraid to refuse, the gatekeeper quickly returned with water and sheepskins. As the three watched in the growing darkness, the animal's grey coat turned to white as the dirt was removed from his now-sleek body.

Just as the sun disappeared, a golden star burst into the sky. The gatekeeper turned and ran in fright as the star's tip touched the lame flank of the horse for but an instant.

Melchior removed the blanket and bridle from the horse he had been riding. Then he smiled at the others and whispered, "It is time to move more quickly, my brothers." He climbed atop the beautiful horse as it stepped surely upon the earth with no limp at all. Then Melchior took his place at the head of the pilgrimage to complete their mission of destiny.

## *the story of* THE ELEPHANT

In a place far from the Holy Land now known as India, elephant herds inhabit lush jungles, moving about the land in orderly fashion. But when monsoons bring torrential rains, even animals as large as elephants have difficulty staying together. It was on such a spring night that a male elephant calf lost his herd.

When morning arrived, the land shimmered with water-soaked greenery as the small elephant stood, confused and uncertain. He walked in the direction of the sun, but found no sign of his family. On the second morning, he strode the other way. By the third day, he realized that following the sun would lead him nowhere; he would have to take care of himself from that day forward.

Before too long, he was captured by a wily maharajah intent upon increasing his personal menagerie. The maharajah's trainers were skilled at their job. They used food and threats to domesticate newly captured animals, but this little elephant would not be tamed. Though punished by the animal keepers, he would not respond to the commands of the humans. A streak of independence ran deep in his soul… until late one day in winter when he found himself face-to-face with a man whose head was wrapped in swirls of cloth. Despite his white facial hair and troubled brow, the elephant felt no fear of this man. He knew the stranger was not one of the maharajah's trainers.

"Come close to me," the human said gently, extending an open palm so the elephant might see that he held no weapon. The animal sniffed the air, examining the man intently. Then he bent his front legs down upon the earth as the man came closer and spoke into the creature's ear.

"I have a long journey to make to a land that has never seen an animal such as you," the man said quietly. "I have been awaiting a sign that our Messiah has come. When that sign comes, I will need a brave companion to help me travel. They tell me you cannot be tamed yet my heart tells me they are incorrect. I believe that God has kept you safe and strong, awaiting this day."

Without hesitation, the now-grown elephant arose and dipped his head toward the splendidly robed king. The man unlatched the pen restraining the "untrainable" beast and turned in silence. Without another sound, the elephant followed the man toward a clearing filled with the glow of the setting sun.

*the story of*
# THE CAMEL

**B**uying a camel in the Holy Land thousands of years ago was no easy task. Breeders saved the best animals for the rich while the poor were offered those with little hope of living to old age. Such a camel was sold to a family of merchants living many days west of the city of Bethlehem.

How difficult her first year was! The little camel's back sagged under the weight of many burdens, yet she never let her master hear the sound of relief as bundles were taken from her back. She grew accustomed to her role and never complained; however, that could not be said about her owner. Every day he complained: She was not big enough. She could not carry as much as other camels. How he complained!

It came to pass that a stranger with skin the color of night arrived from the west. Townsfolk murmured about the royally robed man with the turban of a nomad and jeweled feet. But though his figure was imposing, his needs were understandable to all: his camel had grown too frail to finish their journey to Bethlehem.

The stranger strolled the market looking for a new animal, but found none to his liking. Just as he began to despair, he encountered an angry merchant screaming like a fishwife as he stacked enormous rolls onto his camel's back. The black man could not imagine that much weight on the little animal and spoke quietly to him: "Your camel is too small to carry your burden."

"Mind your business, stranger," the man shot back, resentment in his voice. "This is my camel to do with as I wish just as your beasts are at your royal command."

The stranger looked at the camel and felt a stirring in his heart. "Sell me your camel. I will give you what you ask."

The man laughed and continued to load, calling out an amount one might pay for a finely bred camel. When he heard the tinkle of gold, he stopped at once.

"Here is your price," the stranger said quietly. "May I help you remove these parcels from my camel?"

At last, the camel was free of her burden. Her new master walked her toward the inn, tethering her beside his aged beast. He transferred a beautiful blanket onto her back, fastening a bridle with tassels of gold. The black king mounted his new camel proudly, continuing his journey to Bethlehem with the other animal in tow.

## *the story of*
## THE BETHLEHEM BIRDS

Once there was a flock of birds living on the grounds of an inn in the city of Bethlehem. They provided early wakeup calls and fresh eggs for the owners and guests.

One cold night in the stable the flock was awakened by visitors — a man and a woman. They were watching their preparations with curiosity when an angel appeared.

"A wonderful gift from God is to come tonight, and the Lord God has given you a voice to celebrate the Savior's birth!"

Blending their new voices, the duck, goose, hen, rooster and turkey sang a sweet serenade to the Child Jesus.

## *the story of*
## THE DOG

Abram and Abra's father would not hear of them getting a dog. So when a stray found his way to their house, the twins hid the pup outside the village. They fed and played with him in secret.

Checking on the dog one cold night, they discovered their pet missing. Abram and Abra searched through fields and groves until a shining star lit the heavens and a band of angels sang beautiful songs. Awed, they returned to their house. By now it was dawn. Waiting for them was their father, with his arm around their flaxen-haired dog.

## *the story of*
## THE GOAT

Joseph and Miriam's herd of goats had dwindled to only one male and one female. There was no money to buy more animals. How could they continue their life as goatherders?

Joseph went into the foothills to pray. Worried and tired, he fell asleep in a shallow cave. He awoke to find his two goats had trailed him and lay at his feet.

Then a star burst forth and angels sang out, "All creatures of the earth shall be fruitful and multiply." Joseph knew this was a sign. That spring, kids frolicked beside his pair of goats.

All photos are
official 5" figures
of

and are imported
from Italy
exclusively by

# INDEX

## Holy Family
- The Holy Family ............ 9
- Baby Jesus .................. 10
- Mary .......................... 11
- Joseph ........................ 12

## Angels
- Gloria Angel ................ 13
- Heraldic Angels ........... 14
- The Standing Angel ...... 15
- The Kneeling Angel ...... 16

## The Three Kings
- The Three Kings' Journey ........ 17
- Balthazar .................... 18
- Gaspar ........................ 19
- Melchior ...................... 20

## Shepherds & Villagers
- The Shepherd Choir ...... 21
- Aaron .......................... 22
- Abigail & Peter ............ 23
- Abraham ...................... 24
- Ariel ............................ 25

- Asa .............................. 26
- Caleb .......................... 27
- Daniel .......................... 28
- David .......................... 29
- Deborah ...................... 30

- Eli .............................. 31
- Ephraim ...................... 32
- Ezra ............................ 33
- Gabriel ........................ 34
- Jareth .......................... 35

- Jeremiah ...................... 36
- Jeshua & Adin .............. 37
- Jethro, Tamar & Saul .... 38
- Joel ............................ 39
- Joshua ........................ 40

- Josiah ........................ 41
- Judith .......................... 42
- Levi ............................ 43
- Malachi ........................ 44
- Micah .......................... 45

- Michael ........................ 46
- Miriam .......................... 47
- Mordecai ...................... 48
- Nathan ........................ 49
- Rachel .......................... 50

- Reuben ........................ 51
- Samuel ........................ 52
- Seth ............................ 53
- Zachariah .................... 54

## Animals

### of the Manger
- The Seated Camel ........ 55
- The Sheep .................. 55
- The Ox ........................ 56
- The Donkey .................. 57

### of The Three Kings
- The Horse .................... 58
- The Elephant ................ 59
- The Camel .................... 60

### of the Village
- Bethlehem Birds ............ 61
- The Dog ...................... 61
- The Goat ...................... 61